LIFE IS SHORT

DON'T BLOW IT!

FINDING SUCCESS
AT WORK AND AT HOME

*

SUSAN GEORGE

*

SERVICE EXCELLENCE, INCORPORATED

NEW JERSEY 2000

"LIBRARY OF CONGRESS CATALOG NUMBER"

99-93754

ISBN 0-9672995-0-0

COPYRIGHT MAY 1999

PUBLISHED BY SERVICE EXCELLENCE, INC. 2000

EDITED BY: Joseph Schwarze

Contributing editors: MELISSA ANDERSON, MIKE GEORGE,

KELLY GEORGE, MICHAEL GEORGE JR.,

MARYANN MARCHETTI, MARGY SOLE

*

LIFE IS SHORT

DON'T BLOW IT!

FINDING SUCCESS AT WORK AND AT HOME

BY SUSAN GEORGE

To: Michael my Love and my Rock

Gina my Courage

Mike my Heart

Kelly my Spirit

To Lois
who has the wisdom
to listen to her heart
may joy fill your days
and peace your nights
Joseph Schwarz

FORWARD

This work is in memory of Mom.

She taught me by her example, the meaning of unconditional love.

She taught me what was possible. Without her gift, I would have no way of knowing the power within.

She taught me I could do or be whatever I wished and nothing would cause her to love me any less.

She taught me of the warmth, the light, the splendor of this kind of love, and because she gave it to me so simply, so freely, so naturally, I knew that God too loved me completely and unconditionally.

TABLE OF CONTENTS

THE RESPONSIBILITY

FREEDOM, HAPPINESS AND HEALTH

PLAN FOR A HEALTHY LIFESTYLE
DESIGNING YOUR CUSTOM DIET
EATING LESS AND ENJOYING IT MORE
YOUR DAILY BURN
GOOD WORK ENCOURAGES GOOD HEALTH

THE PEACE

MEDITATION MADE SIMPLE

THE POWER OF YOUR BREATH
EAST MEETS WEST – ZAZEN

THE JOY

BUT ARE YOU REALLY HAPPY?

BALANCE YOUR LIFE WITH WHO YOU LOVE
MAKE JUST ONE SOMEONE SMILE
ACTIVE PHILOSOPHY VS PASSIVE PHILOSOPHY
LET GO OF RESENTMENT
ALL MAJOR RELIGIONS
GOOD TO KNOW YOU ARE NOT ALONE

THE BEGINNING

MISSION STATEMENT

DAILY PRAYER
LIST OF REMINDERS
BOOKS TO READ ALONG THE WAY
CONCLUSION

"If you want to know

who you are…

You have to spend

some time with yourself."

Unknown

INTRODUCTION
THE FIRST DAY OF YOUR LIFE

What you think and believe is what manifests in your life. Taking responsibility for the quality of your life and the direction of your future life will be a most enjoyable and challenging journey. This book is designed for the individual who has made a decision to take control of his or her personal growth and embark on a journey of self-actualization.

Using this book as a tool, you will become more aware of the power within which can create the reality of your life. You will discover your passions and overcome barriers which have blocked your performance in the past. You will connect more deeply with your spiritual center and learn to live from a place of joy and inner peace. You will open up new areas of creativity and choice and awaken as never before.

I expect that by the end of this book, as you follow the steps and take the time required, you will discover more fully the potential of your body, mind and soul. You will undoubtedly make your career and your relationships more meaningful than you had ever before dreamed possible.

This book puts into action the ideas of some of the great thinkers of our world past and present. You will hear from Plato, Jesus, and Buddha. You will listen to the words of Augustine, Einstein, Emerson, Gibran, Goethe, Kafka, Lao-Tzu, Merton, Rumi, Schweitzer, Sophocles, Suzuki, The Dalai Lama, Thoreau, The Tao, Hindu Texts, Hebrew Texts, Christian Texts and many more. All of these great thoughts are united before you as an offering to better prepare yourself for the new millennium.

"The journey of a thousand miles begins with a single step."

Lao Tzu

THE PURPOSE

"To know what you prefer
instead of humbly saying 'amen'
to what the world tells you
you ought to prefer is to have
kept your soul alive."

Robert Louis Stevenson

WHAT IS YOUR PURPOSE?

Who are you and what is your purpose?

Ask yourself this question and begin to consider that you are much more than you think yourself to be.

You are love and light and truth and beauty. You are power and strength and compassion and mercy. You are joy and generosity. You are all of the highest ideals that you can begin to imagine, and more than your most fantastic daydreams would have allowed you to believe. This is who you are and have always been, but have perhaps forgotten.

The poet Rumi reminds us that, *"When you see your true beauty, you will be the idol of yourself."*

To begin the search to find your true beauty, I want you to think of your unique self as an acorn that has lain dormant it's entire life. This acorn has been unable to grow and mature to its full glory and splendor due to malnutrition. It will begin to develop and ripen as it feasts on nutrient-rich, self-exploration, knowledge, and love.

This acorn is who you truly are, and each day you grow to become more of who you are. The essence of you, however, is already there in its totality, buried deeply inside under all of your hopes, fears, thoughts and desires. Your challenge is to cultivate this essence into the magnificent oak which you were born to become.

Let me begin by telling you what caused me to question who I am and what my purpose is.

In the early eighties I was working for a multi-unit retail operation in New Jersey. The Chief Executive Officer of the company was newly transferred from Japan. As part of his orientation he was traveling nationwide meeting the managers of his operation and visiting their areas of business, assessing the condition of his company.

He sat down to have a conversation with me, one-on-one, to get to know who I was and what I was all about as part of this process.

I prepared for this two hour visit by cramming every piece of information into my head I could possibly absorb. I memorized facts and figures in each profit and loss statement about all of my business units. (There were fifty at the time.) I studied the competition and had materials available for the CEO to review if needed. I was responsible for over one hundred people including managers, supervisors, maintenance personnel, drivers, secretaries, and front line sales associates. I spent days preparing for this meeting and at the critical moment I was left without a single idea of what to say in answer to this man's very first question.

Yoshi sat across from me in my office, looked into my eyes and asked me, "Susan, what is the purpose of your life?"

There I sat like a complete idiot. I did not move I was frozen in my chair and stared at him as if paralyzed by an invisible ray gun. My mind was a total void. A vacuum. But thankfully, nature rushes to fill a void and the honorable Yoshi rushed to fill mine. Although it seemed like an eternity that I sat there in silence, I am certain that the actual time was something less than an hour. Yoshi rescued me by sharing the purpose of his life.

He told me he'd made a conscious decision to build his life based on his personal values. His purpose, he said was to give every opportunity possible to his family. He wanted to give his children the best education to prepare them for life. He wanted to spend time traveling all over the world with his family and enjoy them as they discovered this planet. This was his purpose, and he had to find a way to make it a reality. He decided the kind of work he would have to do to accomplish this task and once pointing himself in the correct direction, he would press on to make his purpose a reality. He told me how well his plan had worked for him and his family. He said that without first understanding his values and purpose, the life he was meant to live would have never come to pass. Our most unusual and enlightening conversation followed.

My new life had just begun.

Here I was in my late thirties with perhaps half of my life behind me and I hadn't even answered the most basic of questions. In fact it was a question I had never even sought to answer. What is the purpose of this life I have been given? The answers to all other questions and controversies now seem to pale in the light of this most awesome and powerful challenge.

Why am I here and what am I to do now that I have finally realized that there is a reason for my existence (beyond going to work every day, earning a living, coming home and getting my family ready for bed in the evening.) The question, of course, which begs to be asked is; "Is that all there is?" The answer which I now hear loud and clear is: "My God I certainly hope there is more!"

How can I take another breath much less make another decision which could impact the lives of a hundred people if I don't even understand this most basic and significant of all questions?

That moment became the beginning of my own journey of self-discovery and nourishment of the acorn within. Finally in my thirties, with hopefully more than half of my life still ahead of me; I began asking myself some tough questions and would not be satisfied until I had found the answers which were right for me.

I do not wish to return to my youth and the time before I was forced to awaken. I have often thought much about this question of purpose over the years. The answer has evolved and changed. I now understand my purpose is constantly moving and growing. My purpose is fluid and not etched in stone like other things in life. It is evolving always and forever flowing and moving like a river.

The purpose of my life today is an infinite journey toward The Good, working to continuously improve who I am. Through both knowledge and love I can progress on this path. I can make progress on my journey toward The Good by helping others to see their own light.

We have each been given special gifts, which make us as unique as a snowflake. No two of us are alike. We each have our own special beauty, purpose and task to fulfill while we are here on this earth. Our challenge is to uncover more and more of the gifts given us by our Creator. It is like peeling an onion one layer at a time. We are constantly unwrapping this magnificent creation. As we journey, and come closer to the goodness in all of us, our beauty becomes more apparent.

Just as an artist is part of his or her creation so too is our Creator part of His creation. There is part of the Divine within every human being. Unfortunately many of us are unaware of our true nature. The journey of life takes us on a pathway of discovery, winding our way 'round and 'round learning more about ourselves as we go along.

... *"One day to return to where we began, only to see the place for the very first time."*

Emerson

Much of our lives are lived like a Tibetan Barto, a process of preparing for one of the four stages of existence; birth, life, dying and death. We plan and prepare, yet never actually become what we were created to be. We say, "I'll live the life I was meant to live after I finish this or that or the other thing." We behave as though we have all the time in the world (as if wishing it made it so). But the truth is, we don't have all of the time we wish. And we need to realize this today. It is time to awaken! We must not waste another moment of this precious life.

This awakening can be awesome in its power and inspiration. The time arrives when you have to create a new beginning for yourself, a new birth. And begin to live the life you were destined to live. Not tomorrow, not next week, not next month, not next year, not five years from today, but **now**.

Our lives need not be only productive. They can also be beautiful, fulfilling, and enchanting, on the highest possible plane; because that is where we belong. We have been created as most magnificent beings whose grandeur no one could reject. Our core, our source, is pregnant with love and compassion. If only we recognized the greatness of who we really are.

Your task is not to try to conquer nor control life, but to look for ways to be one with it. Follow the signs that lead you to where you are intended to be.

*Who are you?

Answer this by saying, "I am...

13

If we are to fully experience who we are we need to also understand: "What is our purpose in this life?" What could be worse than knowing who we are and not having the ability to experience that which we were created to be?

*What is the purpose of your life?

Take a moment and reflect on the question, before you commence on this journey.

Write your thoughts on your purpose as you now understand it. Do not be too concerned if you are uncertain and tentative about your answer. If you are not satisfied with the answer you have given yourself; know that you are doing what you can do right now and that the more you learn the more you will be able to do. This is the purpose of our work, to help you to understand yourself better than you ever have before. You will have a far greater understanding of who you are, what your purpose is and how you will be able to work toward being the most complete human being you have the ability to become when you've finished this work.

When you know what is possible for you because of who you are, your entire world will explode with what can now be. When the blinders are removed and you can see the reality beyond this physical world your power will be released and you can begin to fulfill your purpose.

"What lies behind us and what lies before us are tiny matters, compared to what lies within us."
Ralph Waldo Emerson

"…Whether you understand or not, God loves you, is present to you, lives in you, dwells in you, saves you, and offers you an understanding and light which are like nothing you ever found in books, or heard in sermons. The contemplative has nothing to tell you except to reassure you and say that if you dare to penetrate your own silence and risk the sharing of that solitude with the lonely other who seeks God through you, then you will truly recover the light and the capacity to understand what is beyond words and beyond explanations because it is too close to be explained: it is the intimate union in the depths of your own heart, of God's spirit and your own secret inmost self, so that you and He are in all truth one spirit…"

Thomas Merton

THE IMPACT OF MODERNITY

The unspoken expectations of society cause us to be in such a hurry to make money and to perform, we are often drawn deeper and deeper into a life of distorted values.

Our ancestors' daily lives were very different from ours. A few generations ago most daily activities focused on survival. People depended on one another for the many types of support needed to exist. Some would be in charge of the hunting. Others would manage the harvesting, cooking and building. Survival was the purpose and goal of all work. Each individual's efforts helped ensure that others could eat, drink, and have shelter. Today this has changed dramatically.

"I don't know what your destiny will be. But one thing I know, the only ones among you who will be really happy are those who have sought and found how to serve."

Albert Schweitzer

We no longer live with our extended family and we no longer depend on its members to plant seeds and harvest fields for us. We are not responsible for gathering the crops so others can eat and preparing the food for the group. We have lost our sense of the greater community and have diminished the scope of our world to the perimeter of our immediate family or ourselves.

Today much of my work entails sitting in front of a computer for eight hours a day. So then, what is my purpose now? I have no connection with "life", with the "whole": the earth, the sky, the rain, the snow, the sun, the oceans, the animals, the trees, the streams, the winds, the spiritual.

My purpose has become clouded.

"To see a world in a grain of sand

and heaven in a wild flower

hold infinity in the palm of your hand

and eternity in an hour."

William Blake

CONNECT WITH THE WHOLE

Think of what it must have been like to have lived in this country a couple of hundred years ago. Think of existing in the wilderness and living with nature on a daily basis.

Consider the power of feeling the wind through your hair, rain upon your head, or sun on your back. Feel the power of living in the middle of this land whose mountains, valleys and caves have existed for hundreds of years before you and will remain for hundreds of years after you have gone. You are an integral piece of this world. You are at one with your environment and it is at the center of who you are.

Take that image and compare it with where you are right now. How connected are you to the "whole" in your daily life? What you will probably find is that there is little or no connection to the "whole". We are running here and there performing our daily routines without noticing the "whole" and not recognizing all the possibilities within and around us.

19

Take a look at your life and make a decision to connect with the "whole" every day of your life, from this moment on. We are so driven by the current momentum of our existence that this may be difficult. Effective change will require a well executed plan of action. We will work on creating these opportunities continuously throughout this book. Feeling connected to the rest of the world is a wonderful beginning to understanding our life's purpose and finding success in work and home.

"We are united with all life that is in nature. Man can no longer live his life for himself alone."

Albert Schweitzer

Find one hour every day to reconnect with the "whole", and thus with all of the life around you. You are not alone, but an integral part of a creation which needs your participation and recognition. If all you can spare is ten minutes, then start there.

Begin by finding a place where you can listen to your favorite music or read your favorite books or poetry. Somewhere conducive to let your mind expand. This place and time should be one known by your family to be yours alone. Some of you may go outside into a park or a yard for this quiet time. During inclement weather you may wish to try a library or a bookstore. It is crucial that you not be disturbed by anything or anybody. Think of this as time to fill up your tank.

You can even spend this quiet time right in the midst of everything. Look out of a window and focus on what is going on in the world outside. Notice the different kinds of birds or the color of the sky or the types of clouds. Choose to notice the number of people who pass by in a five-minute period, or how many wild animals there are, or how the children in the neighborhood are dressed.

Understanding that we are connected to the rest of the world and that we can have a positive influence on this planet allows us to know that our lives have value.

Think of your connection with the world as if you were a star and your light shines and reflects off of the lights of other stars and moons in the universe. However, without your brilliance all other heavenly bodies would be much less than with your glorious glow.

All day you are giving energy to your work, your children, your partner, as well as your friends and coworkers. Soon there will be nothing left to give, if you don't take the time to go back to the source of life and fill up your tank with the power and energy which is yours for the taking all around you.

If you make it a habit to spend an hour a day re-energizing yourself by going to the source, reading books which excite you, or observing nature; you will begin to see just how much this one little hour will positively impact the rest of your day. You can bring your entire existence to another level by connecting with the "whole" and beginning to recognize the radiance of life.

One evening, sitting in my garden, taking in nature and reading a story about Mother Teresa, I was forever changed by the words on the page. She was asked how she was able to deal so powerfully with all of the constant sickness and death of the poorest of the poor. Her simple answer brought a new light to my life. She said with all of the people she cares for, even with the most grotesque and deformed lepers, all she sees is Christ. From that moment on I began to look and to see so much more deeply into everyone I met. I could see all the way to the center of their being to their most beautiful divine natures. I could begin to understand the power and the potential of the individual.

Your life can be transformed by giving yourself this daily gift of time to explore this new unique world around you. Take the time to open your eyes and really see for the first time what is right there in front of your nose.

"I was suddenly overwhelmed with the realization that I loved all those people, that they were mine and I theirs... it was like waking from a dream of separateness... this sense of liberation from an illusory difference was such a relief and such a joy that I almost laughed out loud... then it was as if I suddenly saw the secret beauty of their hearts, the depths of their hearts, where neither sin nor desire nor self-knowledge can reach, the core of their reality, the person that each one is in God's eyes. If only they could all see themselves as they really are. If only we could see each other that way all the time. There would be no more war, no more hatred, no more greed."

Thomas Merton

STEP UP TO A NEW PERSPECTIVE

Perspective is a wonderful thing to study and consider. When you understand the impact your perspective has on the way you lead your life you will become far more observant and awaken to new possibilities.

*Let us begin with a very simple exercise I use in many seminars. Take a moment and look around the space you are currently occupying while sitting down on a chair. Write down everything you see. Write for three minutes. The next step is to sit on the floor and repeat the same exercise. Write down everything you see. The final exercise is to stand on the chair and then write for three minutes about what you see. Now I want you to read your work and see how you have opened up your world simply by moving a few feet. Consider what would happen if you moved more than a few feet...

We are always gathering information and acting on it. But the information we gather is directly related to our perspective. If we never bothered to move up or down a few feet our data would be quite different. Our ability to make good decisions is based on our ability to gather good data. When insufficient or biased data is accumulated the decisions we make may be incorrect for us.

I am asking you to expand your area of vision to include the broadest scope possible. This relates not only to where you are standing, but also to what you are reading and what you are listening to on the radio in the car going to work in the morning, or what you watch on television. What kind of information are you absorbing?

Consider the quality of the information you are taking into your being and consider becoming more discerning in your selections. This also relates to trying something new in your reading material. If you always read novels, try non-fiction for a while and see where it takes you. If you are always reading science fiction then go for a classic. Challenge yourself continuously to see the world from a different point of view by gathering in ever changing types of data.

Consider what it would be like to have lived your entire life in a dense, thick, forest, never having had the ability to see the sun rise nor set (as the view was always blocked by the trees). Think of how you might react to being taken to the top of a mountain where you could see both the starting and ending of every day for the very first time. If you had never before been able to see the horizon and view the great expanse of the ocean; what would your response be after seeing life from a totally new perspective? What would the effect be now having the opportunity to gather in new and different data?

Author Joseph Campbell tells the story of what really happened when a forest dweller was taken for the first time to the top of a mountain and got to see all of the animals in the valley. Because he did not understand perspective, he thought all of the animals were the size of ants. The sight of the vastness of the world now before him frightened him so that it sent him running and screaming back into the forest.

I am not suggesting that you overload on so much new data that you find yourself running and screaming back into your little world; but I do suggest you challenge your perspective frequently. What would happen if you began to see things you have never seen before?

In Plato's "Allegory of the Cave", he speaks of the world as being made up of people living in a darkened cave lit only by a large bonfire. The people are chained to their positions. All they have ever known of life is darkness with the exception of the human shadows on the walls of the cave. They are unaware of any other life forms, of color, sky, animals, vegetation, or the sun, moon and stars.

Plato asks us what happens when one of these people escapes this cave existence and returns to tell the others what is possible? When this person returns to the cave and tells the others about the ocean and waves and the mountains and sun and the moon and stars and the plains and grass and the trees and animals, how do you think they might respond?

*Do you think they would believe such revelations? Put yourself in the position of the person chained in the cave who has never seen anything but shadow and darkness.

Take three minutes to write what might be your reaction to such revelation.

Now put yourself in the position of the person having seen the light. Write for three minutes on how you might tell the others about the wonders you have seen and try to convince them of the reality of it all. How would you encourage them to see the marvels and possibilities now open, if only they would take that one small step into the light and leave the darkness forever behind?

So our work now also includes a search for new perspectives which will enable us to grow as human beings toward our intended potential. By changing our perspective we increase our opportunities to grow and learn. We are now working with a much larger database of information. Decision-making becomes chock full of previously unimagined possibilities.

When we are living within our same small world; we are like those poor people chained to the wall in Plato's cave. We are unaware of the reality of the life around us. Remove your chains by exploring the acorn within. <u>*Listen*</u> *to what the world is trying so hard to tell you if you just open your ears and your eyes to the power within you. Read, study, investigate, question! The answers will be given to you. The search is up to you. Without the search, your discovery of truth may never be made.*

"Listen, my son with the ear of your heart."

St. Benedict

27

"What is life but the angle of vision?

A man is measured by the angle at

which he looks at objects.

What is life but what a man is

thinking of all day?

This is his fate and his employer.

Knowing is the measure of a man.

By how much we know,

so much we are."

Ralph Waldo Emerson

LESSONS FROM LIFE

Let me share with you my own experience and one of my great journeys of discovery.

My husband worked in Manhattan for fifteen years. He made the commute from South Jersey to New York City, day after day. There were days when the trip took an hour and a half each way and others when it took two to three hours. Mike used to say that work was literally killing him; and I do believe he was correct in that assertion. Spending one half of the day in traffic and the other half in a windowless skyscraper was a slow death for him as I am sure it is for thousands of others. Yet he did it for his family. He made the sacrifice for the well being of his family. Or so he thought... But his family didn't get to enjoy his presence, his humor, or his intellect because he was rarely at home.

I must say that not looking from his perspective; I had no understanding of his lifeless existence. A change in circumstance occurred and I too had the opportunity to stand up on the chair in which I was sitting and see the world from a different perspective.

When I joined my husband in the battle of the New York commute to do business in "the mother of all cities", I too, began to lose my life just a little every day.

We would leave the house and our three children at six thirty in the morning and not return home until seven thirty in the evening. How much time did that leave us for the most important people in our lives, our family? After making dinner and cleaning up, we would be lucky to have thirty minutes to spend together. Life went on like this for longer than I care to remember. There was no time for anything or anyone other than our work. There had to be a better way.

To avoid making the mistakes that my husband and I made, one has to <u>know</u> who they are and why they are here and one has to <u>act</u> upon that knowledge. The French call it their, "Raison d'Etre" or "Reason for Being". My husband and I dragged ourselves through our lives. Before awakening we were both feeling completely depleted and very much without a "Reason for Being".

We both felt as though we were beaten. It seemed to us that we had no value, no worth, and no light. But our difficulties offered us a window into our true light, our true value and our true nature. Living this "half life" helped us to see there had to be a better way.

Pain causes suffering which in turn causes us to think, and thinking enables us to find a better way.

Consider the story of a man who, in his whole life, never did what he wanted to do. Sinclair Lewis writes about such a man in his book <u>Babitt.</u> Sometimes we allow ourselves to be like Babitt because life is just not bad enough to do anything about it. Living an unfulfilled life is terrible; but not as unpleasant as the fear of change.

It reminds me of "The Wounded Dog Story". A man walking down the street sees a dog lying on the road moaning and groaning. The owner is sitting next to the dog and a passerby asks the owner why the dog is lying there in pain. The owner says it is because he is lying on a nail. The passerby asks him: "Why doesn't the dog just move?" The dog owner says, "Because it doesn't hurt him enough to get up and move."

Just like Babitt and the dog, we are in pain. Sometimes we are not in enough pain to actually do something about it. We hate suffering but we fear the pain of change even more. Until the pain of the nail is worse than the pain of change; we will just lie there moaning and groaning and make no concerted effort to change our existence.

Ask yourself: "Have I never in my life done what I have wanted to do?" If the answer is "yes", begin today to make changes in your reality. If you can see it and you can believe it, you can make it happen!

You do not have to live the life you were not intended to live.

"It is not because things are difficult that we do not dare; it is because we do not dare that they are difficult."

Seneca

THE SEARCH

CHAPTER TWO

AWAKEN TO THE POSSIBILITIES

FIND YOUR CENTER

LOVE WHAT YOU LOVE

DEVELOP YOUR HIGHER NATURE

"You see things and you say why?

But I dream things that never were;

And I say

Why not?"

George Bernard Shaw

AWAKEN TO THE
POSSIBILITIES

Consider that you may wake up one day and find you have placed your ladder of success up against the wrong wall. And so when you make it to the top of the ladder, you might find out there is nothing there for you. The top is empty and without the value you had originally placed upon it.

Sometimes we end up in this position because we have not addressed the deepest part of our nature. Thus, you may have spent all of your time climbing your ladder of success and end up losing those things which are most important to you. So when all is said and done you have lost your spouse and your children and your health and your integrity and even your spirit to that thing on the top of your ladder of success. All of this can happen if we don't first understand what is really important to us and build our lives based upon those values.

I have a simple exercise that will act as a window of light to help guide you with new thoughts and ideas about who you are and what you really want to accomplish in your lifetime. The purpose of this exercise is to make you think. Make you ask yourself some questions. Make you visualize some new possibilities that you had not taken the time to notice before this moment.

Now before you proceed any further; I want you to take the time to go through this exercise. It will take you as much as an hour to do; but it will be worth the effort. If you decide not to take the time to do this step, you will be missing key pieces of the puzzle necessary to create the picture of your success.

*Go through magazines and newspapers and cut out illustrations that remind you of your pain and your fears. Look for pictures that remind you of your joys and your desires. Glue your pictures on some newsprint and reflect on the collage you have just created. See how you can get a better understanding of who you are and just exactly what the possibilities are for you from your creation.

Don't worry about including too many pictures in your collage; the bigger the better. Mine turned out to be three feet high by five feet long. I had a lot of issues to deal with.

When I made my collage, I hung it up in my office. I kept it there for several months. I would look at it every day and usually see something new in it I hadn't seen before. I would reflect on the reasons for selecting some of the pictures and with each day I became more and more aware of what was holding me back. My fears were visually confronting me every day. I came to a more profound understanding of what I wanted and needed to do to eliminate those fears, and move toward my desires by studying this collage I'd created.

"Even if your efforts of attention seem for years to be producing no result, one day a light that is in exact proportion to them will flood the soul."

Simone Weil

Once I had opened this door to the question of purpose, I began to spend more time alone thinking and listening to my heart. I would sit in my basement in front of my computer and ask myself questions. Question upon question, over and over again until I had managed to write the answer, which sang to me in all of its truthfulness and authenticity. When I had come upon the ideas which were correct for me, I knew it. Once there was no longer a question, I knew I was finally being honest with myself.

This process took many hours of work to accomplish. I finally arrived at the place where I knew I was no longer thinking based upon what was right for my culture or for my spouse or for my friends. *I was finally thinking about what was right for me. What joy and relief I felt! Why is this such a difficult thing for us to do? Perhaps because we have forgotten who we are and we somehow don't fully appreciate our individual worth and innate value.*

I remember asking myself what it was I valued and eventually coming up with a list of the following things: I valued spending time with my husband, doing things together. I valued having time for my children when they had time for me. This was big, because as children get older, there are fewer moments when they can be with you and if you are not flexible, then you miss those moments.

I can remember after my mother-in-law died, my father in-law came to spend a week with us. Now that I look back, I imagine how terrible it must have been for him. Neither Michael nor I had any time to spend with him. We got up and went to work in the morning, threw together a meal after work, and were too tired to do anything but sit in front of the television in the evening. My father-in-law died several months after that.

Now I think about how wonderful it would have been if my husband and I had been able to spend that time enjoying him.

When I make my list of things I value; time is a big one. Time for the people I love. Another important issue for me is doing work that I love. Having time to spend in quiet reading and meditating and exploring the spiritual side of who I am also made it on my list. Finally, I decided that I must make time for keeping my body in shape. If I continued doing what I had been doing I would most certainly find myself sick and failing. I had created much of my former illnesses by eating poorly, never exercising, smoking two packs of cigarettes a day, and working in a high stress environment.

Once I had gotten this list of values together I began investigating how I would manage to get my life from where it was to where it needed to be. I found that one of the biggest reasons I wasn't doing what I wanted to be doing with my life was simply because I had never taken the time to think about it. The other reason was fear.

So many fears I came to realize. Fear of failure, fear of success, fear of not being loved, fear of loss of security, fear of fear, and on it went. So part of my work would be learning how to overcome all of the fears I had managed to create for myself over the years.

I decided to work through a funeral exercise and see what insights would come from doing that. I sat in my basement visualizing that my death was here and I was lying in my coffin. This was the time for me to review my entire life. I listed all of the regrets I had accumulated over the years and began to understand that life in this form is not forever. If I kept on living as I was, I would find myself in a real coffin one day, buried deeply under a pile of regrets. This was not a pretty sight, but it did awaken me to the work I had ahead. It was time to stop putting off living and start dreaming of what could be, rather than accepting what could not be.

I knew that in order to create the life of my dreams I needed to allow myself to dream as big as I wished. This was not the time to worry about how I would achieve those dreams but the time to give myself the freedom to dream. While working in a dark, dreary, damp and cold basement, with a light bulb hanging from the ceiling, I dreamed the biggest dreams I had ever dared to dream!

"Learn to listen. Opportunity could be knocking at your door very softly."

Frank Tyger

I wanted work which allowed me both creativity and flexibility. I wanted to be able to be with my husband when he had a day off. When my children came home for a visit, I wanted to be able to spend time with them. So I began to look at all of the work that lent itself to that kind of flexibility. I made lists of the different kinds of jobs fitting into my plan.

While I was in this dreaming mode I thought, why not expand the vision to include a home where I had always wanted to live… at the beach. So part of my dream became that I needed to find work which enabled me to live by the sea, while I was still close enough to see my children whenever they were able to visit.

In order to find work that I loved as well as work that would fit into the lifestyle I was designing for myself, I made a list of the things I enjoyed about the work I was currently doing and another list of the things I disliked. My next step was to ask the people I was working with what they thought I did well and what I did poorly. A picture was beginning to come into focus.

The vice president of the company told me that he thought I should become a public speaker and motivator.

He told me that after he had attended a meeting which I presented, he was overwhelmed by my natural ability to motivate people.

The interesting thing was that without his input I probably never would have hit on this particular part of my work because the lion's share of my job was simply, business management.

The advice of Bruce Nyquist was invaluable in discovering what abilities were asleep within me. Bruce died of cancer before I had the chance to tell him that his insight helped to change my life. Hopefully he knows what his good words have done to help me.

I created a profile of this new work I could one day perform. I could give lectures and go on speaking tours teaching about everything I had learned in all of my years running a business. I could teach customer service and total quality management, time management and supervision skills. This kind of work would give me the joy of sharing my knowledge with others and motivating them to seek heights they may not have previously dreamed possible. Of course the best thing about this kind of work would be the flexibility. It would allow me to have time for my family and time for myself while still helping others.

I looked at ways I could begin this new business while still working as a business manager. I had developed a good number of contacts which would be useful to build future business. I would also need to create new contacts and so I began to join groups, which might be in need of my services as a speaker, motivator, and corporate trainer. Slowly I began to get speaking engagements.

I wrote presentations and did a lot of reading to support the work and eventually decided to go out on my own and leave the nine to five corporate world behind. This decision was difficult because I truly loved my job and the people with whom I had the pleasure to work. But our organization was in a state of flux and the writing on the wall was telling me that much of what I loved about the work would soon be eliminated. The most important thing to me about my job was that I had the ability to be creative and take risks using this freedom to explore what the best possible ways of doing business might be. Without that I knew I would no longer love the work.

In addition to the connections I had managed to make over the years; I decided to find an agent to help me to obtain work. That was the key to replacing some of the income I had come to rely on after working for the same company for thirteen years.

The new career was going well. I loved spending time working at home doing research for my seminars. When my preparation was completed I got to travel all over the United States and even managed to do a speaking tour in Europe. It was wonderful but I still needed to live by the sea to make my dream complete.

Ten years passed. Last year the dream came true and my husband and I moved across the street from the ocean. Now my dream of walking the beach every morning is a reality and my husband and I have time to spend together. When my children come home I am with them. Life is good, and joyful and beautiful! I know now that it can begin to give you what you ask of it if you take the time to plan and act on those plans accordingly.

I have given you this piece of my story so you will begin to understand why I am so passionate about what is possible. It is possible for you as well.

"For the things we have to learn before we can do them. We learn by doing them."

Aristotle

"If you have built castles in the air,

Your work need not be lost;

That is where they should be.

Now put foundations under them."

Henry David Thoreau

FIND YOUR CENTER

The Dalai Lama shares with us his purpose: *"We are visitors on this planet. We are here for ninety, a hundred years at the very most. During that period we must try to do something good, something useful with our lives. Try to be at peace with yourself and help others share that peace. If you contribute to other people's happiness, you will find the true goal, the meaning of life."*

Notice that the Dalai Lama emphasizes the meaning of life as relational in nature, finding your own peace and sharing it with others. This certainly seems simple enough, and yet the search for this goal takes us on a complex journey into the nature of ourselves and humanity.

When I was very young and getting ready for college I felt that my center was in the Arts, for that is where most of my energy went when I could enjoy my own private time. My father said there would be no art school for me because there was no money in that. With this edict I was off to the university. And so instead of spending these years exploring what brought me joy; I spent much of my time in many areas which held no interest for me. Maybe you had similar experiences which forced you from your center into a different direction.

Because life is so extraordinary, our center can be found by wandering around as well as by traveling in a straight line. Although one might think a straight line would be far more productive; sometimes the wandering is well worth the extended journey.

As I wandered through my college years searching for my reason for being, I was introduced to philosophy. I had found quite by accident an area where I came alive just as I had as a child playing with the arts.

Again, I did not pursue this area because I didn't imagine it would pay the bills. Continuously throughout my life I have been drawn to philosophy. When all of my friends were reading romance novels I was reading <u>Plato's Symposium</u>.

I began my career chasing after (you guessed it) money. My purpose in life was to make money. That was it in a nutshell. Shallow as that nutshell may seem.

My passion for the arts and philosophy did not die. It remained buried for many years. My reading took me to studying areas of love, sociology, theology, psychology, and compassion. Slowly the picture became clearer to me. I was carving a path toward my center. It may have taken more than forty years, but that is where I was heading.

I eventually began to apply some of the principles I had been reading about to my work and developing a totally different way of managing people than that which had been acceptable for the seventies and early eighties. My work life became more fulfilling, by adding this piece of my center to my economic pursuit.

The following quote by author Joseph Campbell, will help crystallize the idea of finding your reason for being, your center, and the most fulfilling life possible for you:

"Follow our bliss and the world will open up to us and put us on a track which has been there for us all of the time just waiting for us to decide to come over and take part in the rapture of life. There are the waters of life all around us, all we have to do is awaken to them and they will fill us up continuously."

Campbell tells us that he decided to focus on the concept of following bliss when studying the Sanskrit words: "sat", "chit" and "ananda". These three terms represent the "brink or the jumping off place to the ocean of transcendence." "Sat" means being, "chit" means consciousness, and "ananda" means rapture. Since "being" and "consciousness" have been worked with often; he decided it was time to deal with rapture and bliss as a springboard to another level of existence.

The concept is that by following what we love our work

can evolve from where it is today to an area of new and exciting discovery of self-fulfillment and self-responsibility and assurance. The process is nothing less than a rebirth from the ordinary to the extraordinary... finding your source of life, which will bring you onto another plane of existence.

The ultimate end to this journey is a total transformation of consciousness where you start thinking and living for a higher purpose. That purpose will flow from what you love.

"The best way to know life is to love many things."

Vincent Van Gogh

"Where your treasure is,

There will your

Heart be also."

Jesus

LOVE WHAT YOU LOVE

You do not have to push yourself to doing things which are not right for you. You do not have to be perfect in every way or be anything that you were not intended to be. You only have to love that which you love, and by doing so, unleash your power.

Today I find myself in a very different place from what I had imagined. In my youth I dreamed about the arts, but my parents did not support this dream. I made decisions to follow the path of least resistance and pursue a less precarious avenue. Because of those decisions, I found myself working in business rather than in the creative arts and was less than satisfied with the place my decisions had led me.

It was not until I realized who I was and began to accept and appreciate the person I had become, that I was able to move on toward becoming who I knew I had the ability to be.

When I understood who I truly was I began to recognize my own strengths and creativity. I became aware of the joy of life, which I had previously been missing by trying to be who I was not. When I allowed myself to pursue what I loved on a more regular basis, possibilities began to expand and explode before me and the knowledge which had eluded me in the past began to fill this void of ignorance.

People ask me how I am able to take the chances I take in my career, giving up the security of knowing I would be receiving a regular paycheck and risk failing completely. My reply is simple. Following my love, my passion, what God has given me as His gift, I have never been more alive. I have never lived a life with more joy than I do right now. Because I am pursuing this gift of love I find opportunities constantly present themselves as if by magic. I am amazed by the ideas which come to me while in silence. Ideas which answer the questions of the day and solve the problems of my work.

"A ship in harbor is safe, but that is not what ships are built for."

My purpose is clear and thus my focus is strong and laser like. Much of my fear has disappeared because I know the work I am now doing is right and good. It is truth and beauty for me.

I find far more courage in this life than in the life of my past. I am finally on the path created for me from the very source of my being. To be courageous means to follow the heart. The God of the Hebrews taught, "I have put my truth in your innermost mind, and I have written it in your heart."

My life had become so filled with activity that I had actually forgotten what made me smile, what gave me joy, and what God had given to me as His special gift. In order to reconnect with this gift it was necessary for me to eliminate much of the rush in my life and reduce my schedule to just those activities which were absolutely necessary. *In order to listen to where I needed to be, I had to create some quiet for myself.*

It is important to understand that that which we love is all around us, but is often hidden by the "stuff of life" swirling non-stop in front of our eyes. Our job is to work on minimizing this "stuff", which is currently obscuring our vision. We will then see our true nature.

*Now I have two questions I would like you to stop and answer. I am going to ask you to put down the book and write for three minutes on each question and don't resume reading until you have completed this exercise. Again, this book is helping you to put the pieces of your puzzle together, but it will not do anything without your hard work. You must listen to what your heart has to say. So let us stop for a moment and listen to the answers to these two questions:

What do you love?

What will you do with the gifts Life has given to you?

"My religion is to live and die without regret."

Melarepa

Reflect for a moment on your answers and consider if you are beginning to realize new ideas by spending some time with yourself. If you see nothing new, fear not. There are more steps to take before we complete this journey. Keep these and all of your exercises with you to read every time you pick up this book to continue. You will find new ideas to add to your answers, new questions, and new answers to enlighten yourself as you proceed along this path of discovery.

"There are men who lift the age they

inhabit, till all men walk on higher

ground in their lifetime."

Maxwell Anderson

DEVELOP YOUR
HIGHER NATURE

"Living" brings out who and what you are and will be. The longer you live the more life experiences you deal with and the more you learn about yourself. Your task is to cultivate experiences, which will develop the higher side of your nature, rather than the lower.

You have the choice to follow the Good. This choice will determine the course of your development as a human being. If you spend most of your time cultivating the negative side of life you will be missing out on much of what is possible. It is important to work to invest your time wisely - pursuing the positive, the good, the beauty, the light of this world, if you wish to grow into the person you were intended to become.

Consider the impact of the music, theater, movies, and books you are selecting before you allow their essence to pour over you and become a part of you. Consider how taking this information into yourself will be affecting you.

Are you nourishing your higher or lower self? Because we desire information from both areas we need to evaluate our choices. If we live without consideration and attention to what our values are, we may be continuously developing our lower natures while neglecting to feed our higher natures.

If your values are family and love and peace and giving, but you are constantly watching television which deals with hate and violence and greed, what might be the cost to you? If the music you surround yourself with and the books you are reading deal mostly with violence and the dark side of your nature, how do you imagine that will impact your thinking? Is it possible that spending so much of your time down at this level will impact your ideals and cause your doubts to grow and your faith in yourself to wane?

If you value things of beauty and hope and courage but surround yourself with things of pessimism, fear, and despair then that is the direction in which you may slowly lean. You may become one with that environment in which you constantly surround yourself.

In the same way, you may become the work that you do every day. You become what that work requires you to think and act on a daily basis. This can be frightening.

Think for a moment about the careers of some of your friends and imagine the kinds of things they have to think about each day. In many circumstances, left unstudied and unattended, modern man can be involved in a field of work which annihilates his humanity.

How many times have you heard of people in the health care profession tell you they have become cold to the misery and pain of the dying? They have lost compassion for their fellow human beings because of how they are required to do their work.

The word "compassion" means suffering with others. When we see someone who is suffering, and we feel their pain, we are feeling compassion. When we feel compassion, we become more human. Without compassion we are somehow less than human. So what do we become if our work makes us void of human compassion? Are we less than we might have been? What kind of impact can we have on ourselves by paying attention to details and thinking through to the end results of our behavior?

Imagine for a moment you are a defense attorney and you spend your life representing guilty individuals who may go free. What can that do to your humanity? How about if you are in law enforcement and you spend your life looking at the lowest depths of human behavior. How must that wear on your soul?

Even in these extreme circumstances, with the proper reflection and attention, you can turn the most difficult vocations into a journey toward The Good. But you must take the time to reflect and contemplate your purpose and understand it as a methodology for the pursuit of The Good.

Remember you are building from one exercise to the next and need to develop an understanding of the work at hand before moving ahead.

*Write for three minutes about the work that you do and then write for three minutes about the feelings you have about your work.

Do these feelings lift your spirits or pull them down?

How can you refocus your work efforts to lift your spirits?

This refocusing can take an ordinary job to a new level of extraordinary fulfillment and satisfaction.

Write about what your life at work will look like five years from now as though it were already so. Create the vision of your life in the future just as you see it.

Doing this exercise will help you to expand the way you are currently looking at what is possible for you in your work and bring you to a new level of opportunity simply by opening your mind and expanding what can be.

Remember the words of the great Sufi poet Rumi,

"Know o my son that each thing in the universe is a vessel full to the brim with wisdom and beauty."

By thinking about Rumi's poem we can envision the vastness of who we are and what we can bring to our work. When we consider that we are a vessel brimming with wisdom and beauty, then what can be possible for us must be far more extraordinary than we may have imagined.

This thought from <u>Being God's Partner</u>, by Jeffery Salkin will help to illuminate the concept for you.

"A few years ago, a young taxi driver drove me to JFK Airport on Long Island. After a few minutes of conversation, I discovered that Mike had belonged to my synagogue years before I came to the community. So Rabbi, he asked while we sat in heavy traffic, what do you say to a Jew like me who hasn't been in a synagogue since his Bar Mitzvah Ceremony? Thinking for a moment, I recall that in Hasidic Lore, the Baal Aqalah, the wagon driver is an honored profession. So I said, We could talk about your work. What does my work have to do with religion? Well, we choose how we look at the world and at life. You're a taxi driver but you are also a piece of the tissue that connects all humanity. You're taking me to the airport. I'll go to a different city and give a couple of lectures that might touch or help or change someone. I couldn't have gotten there without you. You help make that connection happen.

I heard on your two-way radio that after you drop me off, you're going to pick up a woman from the hospital and take her home. That means that you'll be the first non-medical person she encounters after being in a hospital. You will be a small part of her healing process, an agent in her re-entry into the world of health.

You may then pick up someone from the train station who has come home from seeing a dying parent. You may take someone to the house of the one that he or she will ask to join in marriage. You're a connector, a bridge builder. You're one of the unseen people who make the world work as well as it does. That is holy work. You may not think of it this way, but yours is a sacred mission."

THE JOURNEY

CHAPTER THREE

WE NEED A NEW LEADER

LOOK TO THE GREAT LEADERS

WHAT MASK DO I HIDE BEHIND?

BRING YOUR LIGHT INTO THE WORLD

KEEP ALL THE PLATES SPINNING

"There is a desire deep within the

soul which drives man from the

seen to the unseen

to philosophy and to the divine."

Kahlil Gibran

WE NEED A NEW LEADER

Today our lives, in many instances, leave us void of all spiritual value. We think we have no power. We think we can do nothing to create change. We have no vision of what can be. Until we are able to create our own vision or we find a leader to create that vision for us, we live a kind of half-life. We go through the motions of life but it is devoid of any real meaning and joy.

To search for your essence and follow the path opened to you by listening to your inner being is not an easy task. It is a lot easier to continue to live in an unconscious state never asking the hard questions and never listening to the challenging answers.

A Hindu text says: "A dangerous path is this, like the edge of a razor." When we make the decision to be our own leaders and take ourselves to places we have never been before, we are on uncharted courses. We need to understand that the journey will not be an easy one. This choice should not be made by the weak and the lazy but by the strong and the tenacious.

We can listen to the wisdom of Emerson who shares with us these words:

"These times of ours are serious and full of calamity, but all times are essentially alike. As soon as there is life there is danger."

We need to consolidate our actions toward one common focus, to more easily unite our vision with our behavior.

As leaders, our job is to go on a quest to find our best lives--what it is we have the potential to do for the good of others. Just as the great spiritual leaders each went on a quest to find "the way", so too can we go on a journey toward The Good.

"The search is what anyone would

undertake if he were not sunk in

the everydayness of his own life.

To become aware of

The possibility of the search

Is to be onto something."

Walter Percy

LOOK TO THE GREAT LEADERS

Jesus went into the desert for forty days and came out of that desert with his message. Buddha went into seclusion and found enlightenment. Moses went to the top of a mountain and came down with the Ten Commandments.

All of these leaders went on a journey to find the best direction to be taken. Your journey is no less necessary to find your own personal direction. The Japanese call it hoshin/kanri, which may be translated compass and sextant, or direction and path.

Sometimes we recognize the direction but the path is unclear. I oft' times have no idea what path will take me to where I want to be. So I make my own path in the woods and try to do at least one thing every day to remove some of the obstacles to progress one step forward on my road.

Without an understanding of both the direction we are to face, and the path we are to follow, we are like a cork bobbing around in the ocean of life. When the waves come in one direction that is the route we take. When the wind reverses direction, so do we. We have not committed ourselves to a life without direction, but to a life of all directions. This choice then leaves us with no focus or purpose other than to float. This decision to float through life is perfectly valid as long as this is your conscious decision and not one made by default simply because you are not paying attention.

If you choose to float through life from one wave to the next, then you will never regret the trip. The problem occurs when you awaken one day to find you have been floating for twenty years and regret that you are forever lost adrift on the waves, never to find your own personal direction and path to your true purpose.

Our great leaders have all gone on a journey like yours, seeking discovery of both the self and the whole. Mohammed was a camel master and he went from Mecca every day to a mountain cave. One day he heard a voice which told him to write, and that writing became the Koran, the spiritual teachings of Islam.

What prohibits us from following the example of the great leaders of our world? Only ourselves. All people have the potential to raise the standards for themselves and thus the standards for all those who they touch. You are a leader with the power to raise the bar for yourself and for others.

"Few have the greatness to bend

history itself.   But each of us can work

to change a small portion of events,

and in the total of all those acts will be

written the history of the generations."

Robert F. Kennedy

WHAT MASK DO
I HIDE BEHIND?

---

*We all wear masks. We wear masks of different kinds at various times in our lives. Take a moment and draw a picture of the mask you wear at work. Next draw a picture of the mask you wear at home. Ask yourself why? Ask yourself when you will remove your masks permanently?

Write for three minutes on how you feel about wearing these different masks and how you would feel if you could remove the masks forever and just be who you are at all times to all people.

One of the managers I worked with many years ago wore the mask of an ogre. He had created this mask because of his belief that the personality of an ogre was required. The leadership of the organization operated from the opinion that fear was needed to produce a well-managed environment.

The way this manager treated others was painful to watch. He would humiliate individuals in front of the customers and coworkers without hesitation. This is what he thought was expected of him, and so behaved accordingly. This mask became a part of him, since this was the way he acted every day. Besides draining the life from the objects of his anger; he was continuously draining his own life force. There was no light behind this man's eyes. There was no color in his face. It was as though he had emptied himself of his humanity.

In the same operation there was a manager who rejected the leadership's claim on him and behaved very differently. He treated people with kindness, love and compassion. I thought this was a very inspiring and hopeful approach. I began to learn humane leadership from him. I knew what was possible because I had seen it done with such powerful results. He taught me to ignore the values of the system currently in place and follow my own values, or what felt right to me. Hence, no masks were required. He taught me to be who I was and allow my love and compassion to be felt throughout the organization.

I won't say that ignoring the system was simple. That is just not reality. Going against the flow is, by its nature, precarious; so I warn you to take caution at every turn. However, the alternative, going against your own values can be far more damaging to your spirit, your life, and your future. You just have to take a stand. From a position of strength you can offer both yourself and the people around you the possibility to grow to their fullest potential. This growth will never occur if you are constantly fighting against your own best nature and wearing the mask of another.

The poet Kahlil Gibran shares with us some wisdom of leadership you might want to think about for a while:

****

"All streams flow to the sea because it is lower than they are. Humility gives it its power. If you want to govern the people, you must place yourself below them, if you want to lead the people, you must learn how to follow them."

So what is it we need to be asking ourselves now? Are you going to be a person of humanity even if it means going against the powers that be? I am by no means suggesting that you would want to set out on a mission to change the world. The world is what it is. I am suggesting that you live your own way within the world as it exists, sans mask.

"The best reformers the world has ever seen are those who commence on themselves."

George Bernard Shaw

"If we work upon marble it will perish; if we work on brass, time will efface it. If we rear temples, they will crumble to dust. But if we work on men's immortal mind, if we impress on them high principles, the just fear of God, and love for their fellow man, we engrave on those tablets something which no time can efface, and which will brighten and brighten to all eternity."

Daniel Webster

BRING YOUR LIGHT
INTO THE WORLD

The issue is not that you will save the world but that you will make the world more alive by bringing your light into it. The way to do that is to find where your light hides and then present it in all of its glory to the world. **What holds you back from being all that you have the potential to become is ultimately within yourself and nowhere else. You are the source of your power and you are also the source of your impotence.**

"Use what talents you posses; the woods would be very silent if no birds sang except those who sang best."

The journey you are taking will lead you to discover the possibility of your own radiance and the strength you possess to bring your most evolved self into this world. The power is not from without. The power is from within.

Once you are aware of your own light, you will begin to observe that same light and potential in others. In fact you will often see it in people who do not see it in themselves. (Much like the vice president noticed my gift and changed my life completely by recognizing the light within me.)

The mere act of your recognizing who someone truly is, is enough for them to be drawn to you. You cannot change others. You can only change yourself. By touching you, and seeing your compassion, energy and excitement for what you do in your life; they will be changed from within. Once you introduce an individual to what is possible; they too will begin to see their own potential with new eyes.

Nietzsche said, "Man is a sick animal". His reasoning was that unlike a beast who knows what to do at all times; man does not have a clue much of the time what to do with himself. Time after time I have met people at my seminars who tell me they just do not know what they want to be when they grow up.

Morris West author of, <u>Shoes of the Fisherman,</u> teaches us with these powerful words;

"It costs so much to be a full human being that there are very few who have the enlightenment or the courage to pay the price. One has to abandon altogether the search for security, and reach out the risk of living with both arms. One has to embrace the work like a lover and yet demand no easy return of love. One has to accept pain as a condition of existence. One has to court doubt and darkness as the cost of knowing. One needs a will stubborn in conflict but apt always to total acceptance of every consequence of living and dying."

Give your light to the world. Give the brilliance of your existence to the world around you. There is only one way to do this. Find what you were meant to do on this earth and then proceed in that direction.

"I find the great thing in this world is not so much where we stand, as in what direction we are moving, to reach the port of heaven we must sail sometimes with the wind and sometimes against it, but we must sail, and not drift, nor lie at anchor."

Oliver Wendell Holmes

This brief story literally lit the light bulb for me. It is from, <u>When the Heart Waits,</u> by Sue Monk Kidd.

"When my daughter was small she got the dubious part of the Bethlehem star in a Christmas play. After her first rehearsal she burst through the door with her costume, a five-pointed star lined in shiny gold tinsel designed to drape over her like a sandwich board. 'What exactly will you be doing in the play?' I asked her. 'I just stand there and shine', she told me."

*What are your strengths and what are your weaknesses?

Put together a plan to spend more time developing your strengths and select one area of weakness to work on improving.

"Life is a romantic business.

It is painting a picture,

not doing a sum.

But you have to make the romance…"

Oliver Wendell Holmes

KEEP ALL OF THE
PLATES SPINNING

If we are to fulfill our life's purpose, it is necessary for us to begin by taking a look at the way our lives are currently organized.

This exercise will offer you specific ideas and actions which are necessary to bring your life into the proper order. I say this because so many people will find themselves currently operating in chaos. They are trying to keep all the plates spinning at the same time and are of course constantly frustrated as one plate after another comes crashing to the ground and breaking into a hundred pieces.

Part of the problem is the simple fact that we have too many plates spinning at the same time. We are never going to have enough time to keep them all going. If we don't stop and study our current situation we will continue with this stressful way of life. We will find ourselves constantly sweeping up broken dishes and cutting our feet along the way. Consider all of the people who share our life and the possibility that they too will be injured by the broken dishes as they fall on the floor all around us. Our actions have great impact on others.

*Let us begin this exercise by making a list of the things that are important to us. Stop and take plenty of time to think about this.

Make a list of all the things on which you are currently spending your time. Life is short. Time is precious. These are truths. We should, therefore, pay attention to the things which are most important and let go of those which are least important.

If we had an infinite amount of time in our day and even more days in our lives; there would be no reason to spend it wisely. But this is not the case. Our time flies by and our days are finite, hence the need to bring thought and balance to the way we spend the time of our life.

We realize the impermanence of life when we are faced with our own mortality. Then we begin to see how precious our days on this earth are. We will be working in concert with our Creator to orchestrate the most harmonious life we can jointly imagine.

A year before Gianni Versace, the famous Italian designer and philanthropist, was found murdered on his front steps in Miami, Florida, he was asked by a reporter: "With all of your wealth and acquisitions, what is the one thing you still don't have enough of?" His answer was prophetic and powerful. Words we should all recognize and heed: "Time, I don't have enough time."

"Time is the stuff of life." We should treat time with the respect it so deserves. As Versace brings home the value of the work before us, never forget his situation is no different from ours. Remember the words in, <u>For Whom the Bell Tolls</u> :"It tolls for thee".

Fear keeps us from following the path created for us by our Creator. Think about it for a moment. Begin to realize that you would not have been created with your special gifts nor given the desire to pursue them, if you were not also given the ability to realize those gifts. If you will just stop fighting what is your nature and take the plunge into being your beautiful natural self, you will find the world conspiring with you to make your dreams come true. This happens to fulfill the reason for your creation. The world's energies will rush to assist you in realizing your destiny.

"I must not fear. Fear is a mind-killer. Fear is the little death, that brings total obliteration. I will face my fear. I will permit it to Passover me and through me. And when it has gone past I will turn the inner eye to see its path. Where the fear has gone there will be nothing. Only I will remain."

Frank Herbert

Make your actions reflect who you are, not who you are not and the world will join you in your endeavors as never before imagined.

A Buddhist teacher told this story: *"Someone gave me this glass. I really like this glass. It holds my water admirably and it glistens in the sunlight. I touch it and it rings! One day the wind may blow it off my shelf, or my elbow may knock it from the table, this*

78

glass is already broken. Even as I hold it in my hand I know it is already on the floor in pieces, so I enjoy it incredibly."

In this story we are simply being reminded that now is wonderful, now is powerful, now is all there is. Nothing we have now is forever. It is impermanent and will one day shatter to the floor. Our lives, our husbands, wives, children, friends, loved ones, will all break into pieces. The point then is to **relish** every moment of now which is afforded us. And for heaven's sake make the most of it! Bring every possible joy into your own life and the lives of others.

For us to live our life with purpose we must be certain to match our daily actions with what we value. Only then can we manage to live in the moment and find each of those moments joining together to create the life of our dreams.

Thoreau taught us in his wonderful book <u>Walden</u>:

"I went to the woods because I wished to live deliberately, to front only the essential facts of life, and see if I could not learn what it had to teach, and not when I came to die, discover that I had not lived. I did not wish to live what was not life, living is so dear; nor did I wish to practice resignation, unless it was quite necessary. I wanted to live deep and suck out all the marrow of life."

Consider the meaning in your own life of living deliberately. Living by accident as opposed to living deliberately, is what many of us are doing right now. By understanding the impermanence of this life we can avoid awakening to that fact when it is too late. The idea of living deeply is what we want to consider as we work toward that same mission along our personal journey.

*The question becomes: What do you value in your life? I want you to consider several elements which may be included in the things you currently value. How important is your health and taking the time to be proactive about maintaining good health? Just how important is your career and how much of your time are you willing to give to it? What about furthering your education both formally and informally? How much of your day do you think should be devoted to learning? Think about both your immediate family and your extended family and consider how much time you would like to allocate to them? What about recreation? Is there any time at all available for doing the things you enjoy outside of work? Do you currently have a satisfactory spiritual life or do you need to allocate some time to pursuing this area? How important is money to you? How much of your time do you spend working out a plan to grow wealth?

Answer each of these questions by writing for at least three minutes on each thought.

I have trained thousands of people over the years. Time and again they have told me their stories of how they are living their lives by accident. They simply never considered that there exists an alternate way to live.

Death has knocked on my door several times. Each has been an enlightening experience, giving me a different perspective with every situation. My first brush with death occurred when I was only eighteen years old.

I had been working for the summer and was busy writing letters to my boyfriend who had just entered the army. This was a difficult time in our nation's history because of the Vietnam War. Needless to say, I did not want the man I loved to be sent into harm's way.

I had a relatively small growth on my arm and really didn't think much of it. But I promised my Mom I would have the doctor take a look at it because it seemed to be getting bigger and changing color.

Much to my surprise, when the doctor saw the little thing he became very excited. He removed the tumor and before I knew it I was off for one opinion after another. The first biopsy was diagnosed as malignant melanoma. There followed endless visits to specialists to decide the best course of treatment.

The decision was made to remove several inches of my arm and then go up under the armpit and remove the mammary glands.

Of course fear was motivating my behavior and my reaction was to tell them to take whatever needed to be removed so I could be ensured of living past the age of nineteen.

Fortunately for me, my friend Eileen was a nurse and encouraged me to get other opinions on both the course of action and the biopsy. The second opinion identified the surrounding area as being free of cancer and thus the only surgery would be to remove several inches of tissue on my arm and follow with check-ups every three months.

We were all thrilled with this new diagnosis. I had the surgery and never suffered a reoccurrence.

Although I was very young, there were some wonderful life changing lessons learned from that experience. My plan had been to wait until the love of my life was released from the army and then we would marry and resume our life together. It had made perfectly good sense prior to this event. Suddenly, it made no sense at all. I became ill at ease thinking about the possibility that my love could be sent to Vietnam and we might lose the opportunity to be together.

For the first time at this very young age I understood the concept of living in the present. I totally understood that all we have is now. The past is a canceled check and the future is but a promissory note. The present is cash and the only real thing we can touch.

So, one afternoon in 1968, while working in a retail store, I looked up from my work and was overwhelmed by the need to change what I was doing without delay. I walked out the door and drove home. I packed my bags and withdrew all my money from the bank, (two hundred and thirty three dollars and fifty-four cents). I packed several bananas, some crackers and juice, and hit the road for the army base in Virginia.

I spoke to no one about what I was doing, not my parents, not my lover, not my employer, not a single other human being. I can remember leaving some sort of cryptic message for my folks but that was the extent of my communication.

I had no idea where I was going to find my love on the army base nor how to get there. I didn't know if when I arrived he would even want me there. All I knew was that was where I belonged. To be doing anything else was complete insanity. Michael and I were in love and being apart during such turbulent times was senseless.

You should have seen Michael's face when I finally found him in his barracks. Shock, happiness, shock, joy, shock, surprise, shock, shock, shock. He sent me home on the very next flight and we prepared to be married within the month.

Michael and I were together in two short weeks, and we had both learned a lesson of living in the present moment and not putting off our lives.

Many said it wouldn't last. Thirty years later Michael is still the man of my dreams and we know our decision to live in the present was a good one.

I was visited by the shadow of death once again at the age of twenty-seven. My husband was away on a business trip and I was home with our first two children. Gina was four and Michael three. We lived in a little apartment in a run down part of town and had no family or friends in the area.

I had been feeling rather uncomfortable all day. I just assumed it was nothing more than menstrual cramps. But uncomfortable evolved into "bend over and can't move" excruciating pain. I found myself on the kitchen floor screaming in agony and unable to get to the phone to call for help. The children were both crying over me and asking what they could do.

Gina managed to call my folks. They drove me to the doctor immediately. He was unable to make a diagnosis. Moments after he had told me to go home, I passed out on the floor of his waiting room. The doctor himself carried me out to the car and off to the hospital within minutes.

I had been bleeding internally for a very long time, explaining both the severe pain and fainting. I was very close to death. The doctor said if I had not passed out in his office I probably would have died at home.

I can remember lying on the operating table and feeling like I was going to die. The cause of my illness had been a pregnancy within the Fallopian tubes, rather than in the womb. The fetus had developed large enough to cause the tube to burst. Apparently these emergencies are very hard to diagnose and therefore often fatal.

Because I had lost so much blood I was confined to bed for over a month. I was unhappy with the doctor for not giving me a blood transfusion at the time. He said I would be better off putting up with the long recuperation than taking the risk of possible problems inherent with a transfusion. (This occurred as the Aids Virus was just entering the blood supply and many were infected by transfusions.)

My entire recuperation was spent living with my parents. My mother cared for us. Her loving kindness was boundless. She brought me all of my meals in bed for several weeks while simultaneously running after my children and keeping them entertained. Looking back on this time I am certain that I never gave my mother the credit she deserved for the incredible effort she had to put forth to keep us all going during this most difficult period.

Once again I was made aware of the truth. **Now** is all that we have, so we had better make the most of it.

With every painful event I learn a little more about life and the living of it as well as I can. I am grateful to have been made aware of my frailty often enough to keep me awake. Without these "wake up calls" I would still be sleeping through life and all of its possibilities.

* Awakened to the reality that I will not live forever, how will I choose to spend the time of my life?

What do I hate about my life and when will I put an end to wasting my time with what goes against my very nature?

"Men stumble over the truth from time to time, but most pick themselves up and hurry off as if nothing happened."

Sir Winston Churchill

THE CREATION

CHAPTER FOUR

HOSHIN/KANRI

REGRETS-I'VE HAD A FEW

PICTURE YOUR LIFE

THOUGHT-THE BEGINNING OF CREATION

LISTEN TO YOUR BODY

MOVING FROM THOUGHT TO REALITY

"Everything should be made

as simple as possible,

but not one bit simpler."

Albert Einstein

HOSHIN/KANRI

If you choose to live your life deliberately then your next step is to follow the rules of "hoshin/kanri" where we identify and commit to our direction and our path.

To help you in understanding the value of making a plan and setting your direction and course consider a simple financial goal. If you are currently thirty years old or younger and your goal is to be a millionaire by the age of sixty-five you have it within your power. The direction would be financial freedom and the path would be to save one hundred dollars a month at compounded interest and let it grow until you are sixty-five. Because wishing will not make it so, your only other option would be the luck of having rich relatives or winning the lottery. *Otherwise, "hoshin/kanri" is the way to make your dream a reality.*

What I am suggesting is that the way to an end is through a consciously created vision and path. The use of money as an example is simply that it is easily understood and articulated.

"The real anti-Christ is he who

turns the wine of an original

idea into the water of mediocrity."

Eric Hoffer

REGRETS – I'VE HAD A FEW

Consider, if you will, that today you are ninety years old and you are walking down a garden path thinking to yourself that something is missing. You begin down that long road of regret and think about all you wanted to do with your life. You remember all of the times you said to yourself; "Well in the summer I'll live at the beach." But you never did. "Next year I'll write that book." But there was never enough time. "Soon I'll have time to play with the children." "Before you know it my husband and I will be able to take long walks together." The list grows, until you can no longer walk with the weight of all you have missed. The regrets grow with every moment and there you lay on the path filled with sadness.

Close your eyes now and visualize yourself lying on that path and see the dirt road in front of you and the garden all around you. See the people in your life whom you love and see that they are all gone now and consider all of the time you wanted to spend with them but did not. You were always too busy with more important things... or were they really more important in retrospect?

We work doing something we hate so we can get benefits that we will enjoy when we retire (and may be too ill to enjoy them if we even get to live that long). It's a very strange way to live. It's like putting off sex until your old age. It makes no sense at all. Now is the time to live your life.

* In a study of octogenarians, the top three regrets they had were they didn't take enough risks, they weren't disciplined enough, and they weren't assertive enough. My question to you is, if today you were ninety years old and you continued to live your life just the way you are living it now, what do you think your regrets would be? Put yourself on that path and truly see yourself at ninety.

"This is the beginning of a new day. God has given me this day to use as I will. I can waste it or use it for good, but what I do today is important, because I am exchanging a day of my life for it! When tomorrow comes, this day will be gone forever, leaving in its place something that I have traded for it. I want it to be gain and not loss; good and not evil; success, and not failure, in order that I shall not regret the price I have paid for it."

Dr. Heartsil Wilson

"Be noble! And the nobleness

that lies in other men,

sleeping, but never dead,

will rise in majesty

to meet thine own."

James Russell Lowell

PICTURE YOUR LIFE

We all go through periods of questioning who we are and what we are doing with our lives. Those feelings are there as a guide to lead us in new directions from where we are today to where we need to be, to fulfill our destiny.

Know that to create the picture of your life in congruence with who you are, you must choose the proper colors and textures. You are responsible for the choices you make. If the colors you choose are inappropriate for who you are, then your painting will not yield a life of joy.

The picture you choose to paint with your life will help you to develop your own personal strength and teach you how to use that divine energy to benefit both yourself and all those with whom you come in contact.

Notice that you are responsible for the choices you make in life. Do you know how important that is to you? Do you realize how powerful that is for you?

Consider that if you are responsible for the choices you make there is no longer anyone to blame. This is big! No one to blame.

*If we are to make good choices for our future we must first understand where we stand today. Where have our past choices landed us? To help visualize your current life draw a pie chart and divide your current activities into pieces of the pie based on the amount of time you spend on each of the activities. So if you spend half of your time at work draw a line through the middle of your pie chart. Now you are left with only half of the chart to fill with the rest of the things you do with your life.

Stand back and evaluate what you have done. This chart illustrates the picture of the life you have created for yourself. Now consider if your life picture reflects your true-life values and goals. If you are not now living a life which fulfills your values and goals; then it is time to take action and construct the life you want for yourself.

You are again working in concert with your Creator, crafting the life which will support your deepest ideals, values, and desires. *You have the power of re-creation just as soon as you realize your part in this creative process.*

When I worked through this process for myself the results were frightening. I was able to see for the first time that my life was out of control. I was giving eighty percent of my time and energy to work and twenty percent to my children. There was no time left for my husband nor myself. I had no time for my spiritual, physical, or intellectual development. Leisure time did not exist. There was no time for anything but work and the basic care of my children. I did not understand that I had the power to change this disaster into something wonderful. I did not understand that I was responsible for making this change before it was too late.

I am taking these unedited pages directly from my daily journal to share the power of this process with you. Because of this it wanders a bit. But it finally concludes with the realization that I am responsible for the choices I make to create the life picture I desire.

****

It's Friday the tenth of November and I felt the need to write down what happened to me today because it moved me so. Since my operation back in June I have been suffering some difficult times with my work. After recovering completely I found myself questioning the direction in which I had been heading for the past several years.

So I sat down and put together a business plan to take me to the next step in my work. Nothing seemed very different to me from all of the other business plans I had put together over the years. I have always been very good at planning and then working through my plans. I've never been one to procrastinate or have difficulty making decisions. The entire process has always come remarkably easy to me.

For the first time in my life something is different. I have my plan. I know what needs to be done. And yet every time I get to the point of taking the action which will bring me the business I am after, I stop. I put it off. I get into something else. Weeks and then months go by and I cannot seem to see my way out of this maze.

I sit down again and again and rework the plan thinking I have perhaps made some errors with the basic process but I continue to come up with the same plan. Yet, I am inexplicably unable to execute it. I just do not know how to proceed. I have no history to turn to for this situation. Nothing in my past has prepared me for this. It is as though I am a different person.

I am reading book after book, like never before, searching for the answer in someone else's history. Maybe I can learn from this one or that one. But nothing is working. I continue to become more and more angry with myself for failing to perform what I know I have done so many times before. This should be a piece of cake for me. What is the problem?

I am intrigued by the audiotape my husband brings home. I've never seen him read anything of this nature before. After he finishes reading Embraced by the Light, I also listen to it and feel moved by the message. We are here to learn and grow as spirits and the only thing that matters in this entire world is love. It is not about self and what I can accomplish. It is not about money and how much I can make. It is not about a fancy house or a fancy car. It is about love for every human being on this planet.

My God, it is not about me. And all this time I thought it was. I thought what I was doing was of such crucial importance. But it is not. The only thing that has any meaning at all is the love I have for my husband, my children, my mother, father, sister and brother and for all of the persons on this planet. All of the time I spent at work involved in my accomplishments, away from the ones I loved seems such a vacuous waste of life. What did I miss while making money? I missed an opportunity to give to my children, one that I will never see again.

My eyes are filled with tears as I think through the years of working what seemed like day and night Monday through Sunday. What was gained by all of this running? Was anything of value gained?

Is there a difference between helping your children and helping the people you work with? Do we owe more to our children than to the people at work? So many hours I have given to them and not to my family. Can I possibly be justified in the pursuit of business for all of these years? I had such passion to succeed, such passion to be the best, to improve the most, to stand out among the rest. It was this passion that moved me ahead, it was the passion that pushed me to give so much at work.

When I look back at it I think while I was in the midst of it the focus was making it better for the people in my charge. I always felt such love for those people. It always pained me to see so many of them in difficult positions. So many of them weren't making enough money and life was one heartache after another. I felt so many times that I could make it better for them. I thought I was helping.

What pained me most of all was the fact that these wonderful beautiful human beings couldn't see their own worth and their own value in the world. They were looking at who they were through blinders and seeing only a small portion of what was possible for them. How could I help in my small way to remove those blinders? What would make them see who they really were?

When I began the speaking tours again I thought it was about more than just "me". I thought I was helping others, motivating them to be better at what they do, and to work smarter. I wanted them to learn how to care more about their employees, to really care, and let their people grow and blossom under their direction, (which is what I thought I had done for so many years).

But what I didn't tell them was when you are spending all of your time focusing on how to improve your working environment there isn't much energy and passion left to give to improve your home environment?

Back to the reason I began to jot down these notes. When listening to <u>Embraced by the Light</u>, the author talks about the fact that she had been praying for years in the wrong way. She relates that in her experience, she learned to pray by simply asking God, for he will always answer. So after months of wrestling with this problem of floating with my career and being unable to take the simple steps I needed to take... yesterday, I said a little prayer. I asked for help. I was tired of wandering around, not knowing what I was to be doing. I got the answer the very next day. When I awakened I remembered a powerful dream.

The dream found me in a bridal shop with my eldest daughter, Gina. I knew she was there but I couldn't see her. In a matter of moments we had picked out a dress for her wedding. It was almost a flash of time in which this happened, barely recognizable. Then, the next thing I know it is supposed to be the following day and I am suddenly back in the bridal shop, only this time I am with Kelly, our youngest child. We are about to pick out her wedding gown.

This part of the dream was beautiful, Kelly and I looking at one lovely gown after another. Holding them up and really seeing and feeling how beautiful each dress was. It all seemed so very real; the airiness of the fabrics, the way the light bounced off of them. Kelly selected the perfect dress and I was so filled with joy.

Flash back. Just this very moment as I am typing I think about how my mother and I went to the bridal shop to pick out my wedding dress. What joy the memory of that time spent together now brings me.

So what did this dream mean to me? What made me go to this place, nothing had been happening to make me think either one of my girls would be considering marriage. I couldn't imagine what would have prompted this dream. So I told my dream to my husband Michael, thinking he might have an idea. He did not. I kept thinking about it because it is so unusual for me to even remember a dream that I thought it must have some significance.

Kelly was getting ready for play practice this morning. She was eating later than usual as she had off from school. She asked me to prepare her breakfast around nine thirty. I gave her some oatmeal, a piece of toast and some juice. While she was eating I was doing my exercises and thinking maybe I should be sitting down with her while she eats her breakfast rather then jumping up and down. But I didn't listen to my inner voice. I went right on doing my morning aerobics. While bouncing up and down; I relayed my dream to her and she understood the meaning. She said the wedding symbolism is about growing up. Even though Gina had grown up in the same home as Kelly, I had very little time to spend with her, due to a lack of attention as I focused on my career. I didn't get to truly feel the moments as I had with Kelly. "We seem so much closer," Kelly said. "You're more a part of everything now."

Kelly left for play practice and in only a few moments I began to understand this was the answer to the prayer I had made just yesterday. I am exactly where I need to be right now. I am doing exactly what I need to be doing. The relief I feel is boundless. I feel that I could fly.

* * * *

Even though I knew part of my original plan was to spend time with my family I had gotten carried away with my business and was continuously planning my way out of family time. When Kelly brought me back to center with her interpretation of the dream I was once again focused on my target.

There is a balance which must be negotiated by you between your career and your family. To ignore this balancing act is to risk the most important time of your life and the lives of the ones you love. Take the time to make conscious decisions about your work and the value it has to you in dollars and in accomplishment. Be vigilant in continuing to measure the value placed on your career effort versus the value placed on your personal life. You call the shots and you make the decisions to create the life you desire.

Just last week I was able to relive the dream after having learned the lessons from my past. My oldest child, Gina, is getting married in June. We went to pick out her wedding dress together. Because of the priority I have placed on giving time to my children; I was able to spend the entire day with my Gina. We both relished every moment of going through the dresses together. We went from store to store only to return to the first shop and the first wedding dress. This time will forever remain an important part of our relationship. I understood that I could have missed it altogether had I not learned the lesson of my dream.

Pay attention to what is important to you and know that it is through the people you love and the time you give to them that true joy is found.

"Life is action, the use of one's powers. As to use them to their height is our joy and duty so it is the one end that justifies itself. Life is a roar of bargain and battle; but at the very heart of it there rises a mystic spiritual tone that gives meaning to the whole, and transmutes the dull details into romance. Man is born a predestined idealist for he is born to act. To act is to affirm the worth of an end and to persist in affirming the worth of an end is to make an ideal."

Oliver Wendell Holmes

THOUGHT-THE BEGINNING
OF CREATION

"Believe as if it were true now"- from the Book of Daniel.

* Now that you have given thought to the creation of your life as you want it to be, repeat the original pie chart exercise. This time divide the chart the way you want your life to be balanced. Be certain to give the amount of space needed for each of your values in conjunction with how much importance that particular value has to your life. This new picture will begin to illuminate the direction you want your life to take.

When I did this activity for myself I was made aware of just how absurd my life had been. I had been spending most of my time doing things which had very little value to me. I had been spending relatively no time doing things which were most important to me. This exercise is like getting a whack on the side of the head! It wakes you up to your reality and leaves you momentarily stunned by the truth.

Identify the area which needs to be eliminated in order to live an authentic life for who you are and consider how you can go about taking that action. Consider which value needs to be increased. Having identified that, think of ways you can increase the amount of attention you are currently giving to that area of your life.

"I want to know

God's thoughts,

The rest are details."

Albert Einstein

LISTEN TO YOUR BODY

"One always has enough time if one will apply it well."

These words of Goethe bring us to our next exercise. This will take you about a week to do properly but is worth the effort. I want you to begin now by thinking about when you feel the most alive. Do you feel strong, enthusiastic, awake and alert in the early morning, late morning, the early afternoon, late afternoon, early evening or late evening? Everyone is a little bit different in this area and it is vital for you to recognize where your prime time range lies.

Because how you spend your time is your life. You must ascertain how to better utilize that time. We all have a predetermined clock inside of us. There are certain times of the day when we are most alert and other times when we are predisposed to be less mentally alert.

Once aware of those "up" and "down" times; we have the capability to better plan how to optimally spend our time.

The concept is to spend your "up" times doing work which is demanding mentally and requires serious thought and decision making. Conversely the things you should do during your "down" times are the simple repetitive tasks which don't require much concentration.

During your "up" times you want to be doing such things as writing, planning, or studying. When you are in your "down" times you want to be doing things like, eating, watching television, talking to friends, etc.

To sort out what you are presently doing so you can replace "up" times with mental work and "down" times with less challenging activities, you'll want to set up a simple time chart. The objective is to measure how you are spending your most productive time of the day and how you are spending your least productive time of day.

If you are making phone calls to friends during your most productive time; you are probably missing out on some wonderful opportunities. Likewise, if you are trying to do your most important planning during your "down" times; you are probably becoming frustrated and blocked more often than necessary.

*Create a time chart. List all of the most common tasks you do on a daily basis down the side of a piece of paper. Now across the top of the paper write all of your waking hours. Spend the next week marking your paper each time you do a task so you can see for yourself if you are spending your time wisely or not. Do not wait to fill in the blanks at the end of the day because the information will not be accurate. Rather, fill in the data after completing each activity. It should not take you more than ten minutes a day to fill in your time chart. By the end of the week you will have a good idea of the way you are spending your time. It's your choice to spend your time wisely and invest it or to unconsciously squander it away.

Review your time chart and note the type of activities you are doing during your "up" times and those you are doing during your "down" times. Now reorganize how you spend your time and note how differently you are feeling about the quality of your life. Once again we are finding ways to become the most fulfilled individual we can become. This exercise will help bring you closer to developing that little acorn within, which is the true essence of who you are.

In order to create optimal life experiences we must organize our time, our environment and our activities so we can maximize our potential. When we use our time wisely we discover that we have more and more time to spend doing the things we love. When we get to spend more time dong the things we love we are happier, more fulfilled, human beings.

Some of you may think that you have no choices, that all of your time is pre-determined for you. But I want you to concentrate on what you can change rather than on what you cannot change. Of course there will always be many things which must be done at appointed times; but there is usually more flexibility to your life than you had imagined if you just give yourself the opportunity to discover it.

A friend of mine spent eighteen years of her life in a job that she hated because she left no room for alternative possibilities. When she finally decided she needed to spend her time in a more beneficial way, she changed her job to work that she loves and has truly taken on an altogether different personality. She is happy and fun loving and full of joy where she was once depressed.

Allow yourself to search for and locate areas where you can create flexibility in the way you spend your time. (Even if it means making changes which may frighten you at first blush.) Just look at what might be possible. Don't dismiss what can be without a good amount of introspection.

"The secret of success is

constancy of purpose."

Benjamin Disraeli

MOVING FROM THOUGHT
TO REALITY

---

*There are some steps needed to take you from your thoughts and desires to action and reality. Let us begin by selecting one area in your life you wish to change. Answer the following questions: What is it you want to change? Why do you want to make this change? When will you make this change and how are you going to go about making this change? List the actions you are going to need to accomplish these changes. Keep track of your progress as you move closer to the life intended for you.

Ask yourself, "What shall I do now?" Sit quietly and listen to what your inner voice tells you. Then take some time to write about what you hear. We often spend so much of our lives in a whirlwind, totally unaware of the answers which are being given to us all of the time.

It is not wisdom to be only wise and on the inward vision close the eyes.

George Santayana

After you have decided how you are going to create your new reality, go on to the next goal and write another set of details. Once again keep in mind that the goals you are creating for yourself are based on what is truly best for you as the unique individual you were created to be. Make certain that your goals are in synch with who you are at your core.

"I was sitting on a beach one summer day, watching two children, a boy and a girl, playing in the sand. They were hard at work building an elaborate sandcastle by the water's edge, with gates and towers and moats and internal passages. Just when they had nearly finished their project, a big wave came along and knocked it down, reducing it to a heap of wet sand. I expected the children to burst into tears, devastated by what had happened to all their hard work. But what surprised me instead, they ran up the shore away from the water laughing and holding hands, and sat down to build another castle. I realized that they had taught me an important lesson. All the things in our lives, all the complicated structures we spend so much time and energy creating, are built on sand, only our relationships to other people endure. Sooner or later, the wave will come along and knock down what we have worked so hard to build up. When that happens, only the person who has somebody's hand to hold will be able to laugh."
Harold Kushner, When All You've Ever Wanted Isn't Enough.

So while you are in the process of creating your future be certain to continuously ask yourself what success means to you. Seek to understand the reasons behind the choices you make to better know who you are and what your belief system is all about.

*Write about your successes. Remember that when doing so you want to look at your work and educational achievements as well as your personal success.

While planning for a successful future I spent time working on several very important issues. First it was necessary for me to understand what success meant to me. Was it making it to the top of the corporate ladder? Was it building my own business? Success can mean much more than simply getting promoted, receiving raises and creating wealth. Although those are valid goals; I felt that success needed to be examined in a far broader sense.

I began to examine other areas in my life in addition to the work environment where I could judge myself to have been successful. I realized that I was fortunate to have found success in the relationships I had with my parents and siblings. I was successful in raising three wonderful children, each working to give the world their own special gifts. The long term friendships I had maintained were also a great part of my success.

The more I looked the more I became aware of just how successful I had been. Although many may not call me a great success; understanding my definition of success helped me to see what was possible for me in the future. If I have it within myself to experience success in so many areas of my life to date; then why not in all other areas as well? Success breeds success. But you must first be aware of your true life successes before you can envision what is possible in the future.

THE POWER

CHAPTER FIVE

YOUR GIFT BACK TO THE UNIVERSE

UNDERSTAND COMFORTABLE VS. CURIOUS

THE PLACE WHERE THERE IS NO TIME

THE JOY OF WORK

MIRACLES AT WORK

LARGE SCALE MIRACLES

"All the arts we practice

are apprenticeship,

the big art

 is our life."

M.C. Richards

YOUR GIFT BACK
TO THE UNIVERSE

We were all born creative beings. As children we were probably at our most creative. If you take a group of children and put a dot on a black board and ask them what that dot could be; you would get numerous answers. But if you were to do the same exercise with adults the possibilities for them would be significantly reduced. This is because while taking our journey into adulthood, we have buried much of our natural ability.

There are many reasons why so many of us feel we are no longer creative. One factor is our educational system, which has taught us to accept that every question has only one right answer. What problems do you think might be produced growing up thinking there is only one correct answer to every question? Perhaps one outcome might be that we would give up trying for fear of being wrong.

There are many schools which no longer offer music and art because these areas are considered to be unimportant to the educational process. The truth is that art and music gently channel children to learn the joy of the creative process which once learned can be easily transferred into the more pragmatic areas of thought such as math and science.

To be our most creative selves we need to lose our fear of being wrong. Picasso taught us that, *"Every child is an artist, the problem is how to remain an artist after he grows up."* It is our job to reconnect with our innate powers, for they were given to us by our Creator.

How many times have you heard people say; "If only I knew then, what I know now"? The more interesting and liberating question might be to ask yourself, "What if I could only forget what I know now?" How would I see the world through the eyes of an innocent child in the body of an intellectually capable adult?

Children are able to see what is possible because they have not been programmed yet to believe the word impossible. This is where we need to put ourselves once again. The great musician, Miles Davis gave us this wonderful thought, *"Do not fear mistakes, there are none."* How powerful, to truly believe this statement! ***That which you may think of as a mistake is just a learning tool to get you to where you need to be in order to learn the next lesson of your life.***

Many of us give up before we have begun to investigate a new idea because we cannot believe we have it within ourselves to know the right answer. So we stop the search. We are in effect creating a self-fulfilling prophecy of our own ineptitude.

We have been conditioned to listen to the word, "NO", from the day we were born. How many times do you think a child hears the word, "no", by the age of five? How many times do you think you heard the word "no" by the time you were twenty-one? It's no small wonder we are conditioned as a matter of habit, to say "no" to ourselves. We have been taught to say "no" to ourselves when saying "yes" to ourselves is the way we become that unique individual we were created to become.

We need to say, "YES"! Yes, I will go to graduate school. Yes, I will invest in that new business. We need to say yes, I will buy that new house, meet that new person, go for that new job, try that new hobby, explore that new book, that new computer, that new restaurant, that new hotel, that new route. Yes to even something as simple as I will taste that new food.

The gift of looking at life with the wonder and enthusiasm of a child needs to be recaptured. It is our responsibility to reclaim what is ours for the asking, our innate ability to create.

"Let us not be content to wait

and see what will happen,

but give us the determination

to make the right things happen."

Peter Marshall

UNDERSTAND
COMFORTABLE VS. CURIOUS

We learn from the studies of Mihaly Csikszentmihalyi, author of <u>Flow</u> and <u>Creativity,</u> that we are each born with two forces inside of us. One of those forces pushes us to be satisfied with the way things are and this force tells us it is good to do nothing. It is called entropy. The other force pushes us to be dissatisfied with the way things are. This force causes us to be curious and interested in finding new processes, thoughts and ideas. This is the force of creativity.

Both forces are necessary. Following our more curious nature will move us steadily in the direction of our intended purpose. We must learn to see that which is right in front of us for the first time as if we were newborn babies (innocent of everything that is). In short we need to pay attention!

Consider, if you will, the thought of being at the right place at the right time. How many of you have found yourself at the right place at the right time, but you were just not aware of it? Sometimes you just don't appreciate the opportunity available to you at the moment. The door of opportunity may shut; never to open again in quite the same way.

Think about all of the risks you did not take and think about how your life may have taken a completely different direction had you taken those risks. Perhaps there was a moment when because of lack of preparation or just plain fear, you turned down what otherwise seemed like a marvelous opportunity. It is important for us to recognize when opportunity is at hand. Sometimes we are just not awake enough to know that this is our moment.

Remember, that the more ideas you investigate; the more opportunities for success you will have. It is necessary to scrutinize a great number of ideas in order to find that which is going to work for you. To be creative you must give yourself sufficient time to develop a new idea and not judge yourself too soon.

"Don't be afraid to take a big step if one is indicated. You can't cross a chasm in two small jumps."

David Lloyd George

The more ideas you investigate the more failures you may have. The creative process is challenging.

"Mistakes are portals of discovery."

James Joyce

We can make a life based on our purpose rather than allowing our environment to determine what is possible for us. We need not be "victims".

Just as creative people have the ability to use both sides of their personality so do all of us. We can be either introverted or extraverted depending on the circumstances. We can be both aggressive and passive. Imagine the impact on our perspective if we have the ability to see the world from opposite sides of the fence. We will see more opportunities than those who only see one side.

Some people will see their aggressive side or their passive side as a negative, and will work against a particular behavior. A more productive approach would be to experiment. Try using the opposite sides of your personality to enable you to expand your vision and perspective of the world around you.

*The exercise to develop this other side of you is a fun one. Begin by having your friends tell you what your most predominant characteristics are. Next make a list of what you feel are your characteristics. After you have completed the list, I want you to write alongside each its opposite.

Your friends may tell you the following characteristics are examples of the way you behave:

Outgoing

Loud

Aggressive

Rigid

You would then consider what the opposite characteristics would be.

Shy

Quiet

Passive

Flexible

Now it really gets fun! Take the experiment into the lab of life and begin to act the opposite of what is natural for you and see what develops.

You will find a new perspective from which to evaluate the world around you. When you put out new types of information the world will return different feedback. You will have gained more knowledge about who you are and your purpose.

"Go confidently in the direction

of your dreams!

Live the life you've imagined.

As you simplify your life the laws

of the universe will be simpler."

Henry David Thoreau

THE PLACE WHERE
THERE IS NO TIME

You may spend hours and days and weeks and months following your goals and when you have finished you may still have nothing. This is the down side of using this gift of creativity.

To create something new one needs to see what is possible. One also needs the tenacity to forge ahead no matter what barriers are blocking the path.

The up side of utilizing your creative gift is that you may create something which has never before existed. ***This is the joy of learning to become your original creative self - the inspiration and exhilaration generated when you break the chains of traditional thought and open yourself once again, to a world of infinite possibility.***

To discover something new you must spend the time to solve your problems (never knowing for sure what the outcome will be).

"What we have to do is to be forever testing new options and courting new impressions."

Walter Pater

Business today needs to teach people how to be creative. Rather than forcing people to be the same and to accept rules without question; they need to be teaching people how to think without restrictions. To be creative we need the ability to question as never before. We need to be pushed toward looking at the world with new eyes. Ask "why" and avoid accepting "no" as an answer without investigation! The creative process takes time. To accept "no" as a matter of policy will stunt the growth of our businesses as well as ourselves.

"Only the curious will learn and only the resolute overcome the obstacles to learning. The quest quotient has always excited me more than the intelligence quotient."

Eugene S. Wilson

While working in Central New Jersey one of my business units decided to create the best organization in the entire company. The team put together a project which they named, "T.O.P.S", an acronym for "Team Operations Performance Specialists". They were given the latitude to question existing rules and regulations and write new procedures and processes based on the knowledge and expertise of the team.

The project included various areas: sales, reward and recognition, marketing, training, measurement, and cost control. I think the most fascinating part of this project was to watch the performance of the participants soar as they became more and more involved in this new way of doing business. What made this so interesting to them was that they were part of its creation. They had input into their own future. The net out was an increase in profitability over the other regions of five percent. Since this was already a high yield operation as were the regions to which they were being compared, the five percent increase was quite notable.

The people on the team worked hours on end to create something new. I found the team members working nights and weekends. I watched as they lost all track of time while they were in the midst of creating this new kind of business. *The creative power we each have locked away can be multiplied and magnified when connected with other team members in a nurturing and open environment.*

"Imagination is more important than knowledge."

Albert Einstein

"There is a vitality, a life force, an energy, a quickening, that is translated through you into action, and because there is only one of you in all time, this expression is unique, and if you block it, it will never exist through any other medium and will be lost."

Martha Graham

THE JOY OF WORK

Imagine working every day of your life but feeling as though none of it were work, because of the joy of the creative process. *This ability to be drawn into your work is possible for all of us because we are all creative individuals. We have just forgotten what is available to us.*

So what is the secret of turning something mundane into something enjoyable? The answer is the ability to design or discover something new. Pleasure is derived from this and becomes the motivation for pursuits beyond financial gain.

In an effort to make work as enjoyable as possible it is necessary to first study what makes anything enjoyable and then apply those principles.

Ask yourself if you have clearly defined goals. If you do not then take the time to write out your goals either by yourself or with the assistance of your peers, your subordinates or your boss.

When you are clear on your goals move on to asking yourself if there is a sufficient amount of feedback in the system to assure continuous improvement. If you find there is not enough feedback to ensure you are always moving in a positive direction, then work with your teammates to set up feedback loops to constantly reinforce that the correct steps are being taken.

It is important that you know the challenges of your work are attainable. If you feel that you are not properly trained to meet these challenges; then request and receive the proper training to bring you to that level.

Ask yourself if you are constantly being interrupted. If the answer is yes, then see how you can better arrange your time and space to allow for sufficient attention to your task. It may mean rearranging tasks or reassigning work. You must have the time to focus your attention without constant interruptions in order to succeed.

Dr. W. Edwards Deming, responsible for the manufacturing success of post war Japan is called the Father of Total Quality Management. He taught us that we must be free from fear if we are to produce the highest quality products and services.

Look to your work environment and see if there is an aura of fear permeating the organization. If fear exists then it is necessary to work to eliminate it in order to excel. Where there is fear there is no truth. Where there is no truth there is no good honest information. Where there is no good honest information, there can be no quality products and services.

Finally, it is essential to have enough confidence in the way you work that what others may think is not important to you. With all of these steps in place, you will experience a loss of a sense of time and the work itself will become intrinsically motivating.

*Study your current work process and assess how many of the above principles are currently included in your work.

My father told me work was never "work" for him. It was always "play". He said he never had a day of work where he didn't love what he was doing. Since my father was an inventor you can see how the steps which make work enjoyable would be readily available to him. Finding something new was pure joy for him. He is now ninety-three years old and "played" as an inventor until he was ninety-one. His first book was published this year.

MIRACLES AT WORK

If we are lucky there are some parts of our work that we love. But there can also be parts that we dislike tremendously. Our task is to learn how to enjoy all of our work or at least change it to something we can find rewarding on some level.

While working for a large manufacturing and retail organization, I was fortunate to be given an enlightening opportunity. All of retail management was required to work in the manufacturing plant for one full week. This was to be a tool to better understand the demands and requirements of the production side of the business.

We were each given a job to perform for the week in the production department. My job was to make reprints. I was to do this process for eight hours a day. I had never done a repetitive task before at work and so didn't have any experience to draw on when it came to facing this monotonous activity. I understood what these poor people who did this job on a daily basis endured. The time just dragged by. Something had to be done to alleviate the boredom.

I decided to measure my work using the clock and give myself a goal of how many reprints I could do in a half an hour. I gradually increased the goal until I looked up and realized I had done it. I had made the time fly by. Getting so involved in the process, and concentrating so hard on achieving my goal, I lost all track of time along the way. By continuously challenging myself I made this work more and more my own and improved my skills to meet my ever increasing goals. I found that even in the most repetitive and boring of tasks there can be joy in the mastery of making it your own.

All of the steps previously mentioned to make a task enjoyable were present in this work; goals, feedback, correct steps, challenges, absorption in the work, no fear of failure, and a loss of the perception of time.

*As an exercise to apply this concept to you take several moments and list which parts of your work you do not enjoy. Select one and see how you can apply each of the previous steps to that task.

Write about how you will make the changes needed to improve this work process. Try the new process and see the difference it makes in your attitude about the work. The interesting thing to notice is not only the difference these kinds of changes can make in your work life, but also the tremendous impact they have on the rest of your life.

"I bargained with life for a penny

And life would pay no more.

For life is a just employer

He gives you what you ask,

But once you have set the wages

Why you must bear the task,

I worked for menials hire,

Only to learn dismayed,

That any wage I had asked of life,

Life would have paid."

Jessy Rittenhouse

LARGE SCALE MIRACLES

If applying the previous principles can make small tasks enjoyable what can they do when applied to entire organizations? Remember what we are looking to repeat in the work process are the qualities of no fear, setting goals, feedback, correct steps known, challenges attainable, and absorption in the work.

A quick look at one of my experiences will illustrate the point more vividly for you. It is nine thirty in the evening in July, at a hotel in Manhattan. The president of the multi unit retail organization is making presentations at a national management meeting.

After dinner the president rose to recognize the performance of some of his team. He pulled out a toy shotgun and much to my astonishment presented it to me. I guess it was at that very moment I began to consider the possibility that I might have made a mistake in accepting my new position leading our Manhattan operation.

All of my peers were laughing hysterically over the presentation of the toy gun. I somehow felt they were far more aware of the implications of a weapon as a necessity for my new position than I was.

The message was beginning to get through to me. Here I was, a five-foot tall middle-aged woman from New Jersey, being thrown to the wolves. The Manhattan area was not only the largest sales area in the country, it also held the distinction of losing the most money in the organization's history.

On my first day I was greeted with news of an armed robbery. The week before my entire office staff had been herded into the bathroom and told to strip naked and not come out for half an hour. The word was that my new administrative assistant was in her birthday suit in record time. All were duly impressed with both her dexterity and speed.

"Welcome to New York you Jersey hayseed! What are you going to do to help us?" And so it began.

I invited all of my managers and supervisors in for a briefing on the current conditions in the city. I was overcome with the severity of the problems. I can still see the face of my youngest supervisor as she burst into tears while telling me what it was like to have a gun placed firmly upon her forehead. This had happened to her thirteen times within a two-year period. What do you say in response to such terror? All of the horror stories began to pour forth, one after the other, until my head was spinning.

As if this were not complex enough, I was dealing with a multi unit organization. All of the supervisors, managers, and front line staff were operating in thirty-eight different locations from downtown in the Twin Towers to as far uptown as Ninety Second Street. My office was located in the eye of the storm on Forty Second Street in the Lincoln Building.

There were armed robberies. There were rats big enough to saddle-up and ride. There were roaches aggressive enough to take over the organization. The shrinkage was the size of the national debt. The employees were burnt to a crisp. No necked brutes threatened to break the legs of my maintenance men. Store managers showed me the guns they kept under their desks. Sales associates lived in their stores. Offices and retail outlets were dirty, ripped, torn, dangerous, and falling to pieces. Yes, we were having fun now! I knew for certain this wasn't Kansas. I understood the reason the president had given me the gun. It was to shoot myself!

After having met all the staff, visited all of the locations, and listened to all of the people; I decided that before I took any action I would call the corporate audit department. Their job was to supply me with facts and figures I would need to begin the recovery process.

Remember previously I wrote about getting a new perspective and gathering in as much information as possible in order to understand where you are? Just as this step is needed to properly plan your personal improvement process, it is also needed to properly plan an organizational improvement process.

Unfortunately, after the data had been gathered, the results were even worse than I had anticipated. The standard level of shrinkage in this business is under two percent and this area had a ten percent shrinkage rate. This meant we were losing huge amounts of money to theft and sloppy paperwork. I had been told by the leadership to "fire the whole lot of them", front line people, supervisors, and managers alike. I believe the terminology was: "They are all thieves and incompetent lightweights."

Just as I stepped on board this sinking ship there were also changes at the corporate level. A Japanese company had just purchased the organization. Enter Shigeru Suzuki, new Chief Executive Officer. Before I had even gotten my toes wet "Shig" showed up at my doorstep wanting to see what was going to happen to the highest volume area in his new company.

He was not much taller than I. This was the only time I have found my vertically challenged body to be an asset. Shig bowed to me in traditional Japanese style. He stayed in the very low bow until I returned the same level bow. We were in this together. Just as this was my first trip across the river to The Big City to run a business, this was his first trip around the world to run a business in the greatest of all cities.

The difference between running a business in Japan versus one in Manhattan is like day and night. I think Shig felt the enormity of the task just as much as I did.

His first task was to visit every location with me, all the time gathering data and growing in knowledge of the area and its opportunities. He bowed deeply to all of the sales associates and listened closely to what they had to say. He took notes at every store and in every office and he grew in understanding along the way.

From that point on the mission was clear. These people needed to know first and foremost that we cared. The organization they were working for really did care about them as human beings first, as well as caring about the welfare of the business.

"Caring is the greatest thing, caring matters most."

Freiderich Von Hugel

The area needed to have clear goals and plenty of feedback to and from the people. They had to be free of fear. We wanted to develop measurement systems to know how we were improving. We decided to demonstrate trust and support, reward and recognition and issue plenty of challenges. Once again the same steps were desired here to transform the chaos and pain into order and prosperity. I was being taught how to manage by a pro. I was given complete autonomy to do whatever needed to be done to return the area to profitability.

We collected data from everyone and began with the most urgent needs. We formed cross-functional teams to address issues of shrinkage, sales, robberies, maintenance, morale, training, and administration. We were committed to a turn-around. We planned to affect it with the people we had, simply by training and leading them differently.

We worked to address safety issues first. Systems and procedures were created and instituted to nearly eliminate the robberies. Taking care of the safety of our staff would demonstrate that we cared about them. Addressing and reducing the shrinkage would show upper management that we appreciated their efforts to put this house in order.

The challenge to fix the shrinkage was daunting but within our reach. We decided to hire an auditor from inside our organization since the corporate audit department hadn't had too much luck in our area.

We held open interviews which attracted eight applicants. One of the candidates had been doing occasional audits for the corporate department; so he had potential. Then in walks Ms. Ilene. She was about five four, in her early twenties, dressed in street clothes, and literally glowing with enthusiasm. *(Enthusiasm – from the Greek meaning "filled with God".)*

Where do I begin? She had no experience in accounting, auditing, nor any education beyond high school. She was the most unlikely of candidates, but her enthusiasm was overpowering. I just could not resist this woman's attitude. She said this was her mission and she knew she could do the job. She knew what needed to be done and all she needed to do was to learn how to do it from the audit department. My fear was more for her personal safety than for anything else. She also convinced me she had lived in the city all of her life and knew how to take care of herself.

Together with Ronnie, another incredible member of the audit team, a plan of action was devised and they proceeded to begin the process. Ilene audited one location after another. As she identified the people involved in theft we let them go. It didn't take too long before the numbers started to change and losing stores began making money for the first time.

As it turned out, very few people were dishonest. Thanks to the courage and power of Ilene, the area went from ten percent shrinkage down to less than two percent, the industry average. She did this in less than a year. We were on a roll and everyone was shocked by the incredible turn-around.

We had a very small budget to spend on improving the tattered appearance of the stores but we were able to obtain new carpeting. As the people in the stores began to see management making an effort to build trust and support they began to take a greater part in caring for their work environments as well. Imagine my surprise when I would go to visit a store or an office and I would see the staff had painted and wallpapered on their own! They were going out and investing in their places of business because they now cared too.

Granted there were still some issues which needed to be addressed; but the bottom line was that they were showing great pride in their work for the first time. The power was being released in each of these people. They were suddenly doing wonders both for themselves and for their organization!

Imagine what it must have felt like to walk into a location and see beauty and order instead of decay and chaos. I can remember walking into a store and seeing a wonderful display of artistic photos and the sales associate suggesting that he would put together similar creations for all of the stores. The talent had been there all the time just waiting to be released.

Imagine how it felt to see smiles and hear laughter instead of tears and curses. I thought that this was the best job anyone could possibly have; to have an impact not only on their work lives but on their personal lives as well. These people looked different. They walked taller. Their eyes were brighter. What had happened? Quite simply they now knew what they could do because they had been given the opportunity to do it. They now knew they weren't worthless, but that they were talented, creative, highly productive human beings.

These people had changed right before my eyes. The same people who were supposed to be fired, were now filled with enthusiasm and terrific ideas. They had begun to see who they were and what they could do. They began to recognize their own power within. This was not only a life-changing event for them, but for me as well. *For the first time I could clearly see the power of the individual. The true essence of who they were. No matter how challenging the surface seemed, the interior was beautiful. All they needed was a bit of caring to nurture the acorn within.*

For all of you "bottom line folks", this team managed to increase profitability by sixty percent over the course of a one year period. Miracles can and do happen if you take the time to put the proper steps in place to help those miracles develop.

"Whatever you can do, or dream you can, begin it. Boldness has genius, power and magic in it."

Goethe

THE DISCOVERY

CHAPTER SIX

SEE THE WORLD

MIRACLES FOR YOU

RECOGNIZE THE JOY OF LIFE

YOUR OWN SPACE

"There is nothing more difficult for a

painter than to paint a rose, because

before he can do so he must forget all

the roses that were ever painted."

Matisse

SEE THE WORLD

Plato taught us twenty five hundred years ago that the most important thing we could teach our children was to enjoy the right things. Consider the power of that thought in relation to our society today. What kinds of things do our children enjoy and what kind of things might we want to encourage them to enjoy? Better they should enjoy light than dark, peace rather than violence, harmony instead of chaos, beauty in place of disorder. Better they enjoy creating art to playing video games of destruction. Better they should enjoy participating in healthy sporting activities rather than sitting in front of the television for hours.

We must develop our curiosity about everything, just as a child is naturally investigating everything, if we are to truly see what is right before our eyes. Children spend every moment learning more about the world with each task they perform. Because children are gathering in as much data as possible they are constantly pushing to see what new kind of information they can obtain.

Our son Mike used to climb on top of the roof of our shed and jump off thinking he could fly. He would ride his bike at full speed and do what was called "bail out" because he didn't know how to use the brakes yet. He did all this when he was about three years old. "Fearless" was Mike's middle name. One day while his father was watching him at the tennis courts he looked away for just a moment and

Mike had climbed to the top of a ten foot high chain link fence. No fear. He had nothing but courage and curiosity and youth. He just needed to have the experience, to test the waters, to learn what it would be like. Just as a child is constantly learning, so too can you - if you maintain your curiosity.

"Life was meant to be lived and curiosity must be kept alive. One must never, for whatever reason, turn his back on life."

Eleanor Roosevelt

*Expand your world and explore it as never before:

1. Think about how you can be surprised every day.

2. Write about some new things that will challenge you.

3. Study what makes things work.

4. Look at things with the eyes of a child.

5. Ask about what things are made of.

6. See things for the very first time.

7. Try **listening** to people.

8. Surprise someone you care about every day.

9. Say something you never had the nerve to say.

10. Find a new way to get to work.

11. Break away from your routine.

12. **Keep a daily journal. (This is perhaps one of the most important steps in discovering your hidden potential.) Don't delay. Begin today!**

Again you will find in paying attention to the world around you and developing new perspectives, new opportunities will arise for you. *Increase the quality and the quantity of information coming into your world and you will increase your ability to self-actualize. Look to see the world as a child sees it and windows will open and light will flood into your being.*

"The true mystery of the world

is the visible,

not the invisible."

Oscar Wilde

MIRACLES FOR YOU

Follow what interests you and spend as much time as you possibly can becoming more knowledgeable on those subjects. You can begin to discover your most divine potential by taking the time to investigate those things which naturally attract you.

A most important thing to remember is that every day holds in it the opportunity for something exciting to occur. At night before you go to sleep I want you to think about what tomorrow can bring for you. Think about what you have to look forward to tomorrow when you awaken. If you are unable to find anything - then create something for yourself.

*Take three minutes and write about what you are going to look forward to tomorrow. In the morning when you are about to get out of bed, think again about what you have written and how excited this makes you feel.

Since I have begun my new life, I truly feel the excitement of getting out of bed every morning because I know there are always going to be new things to learn. Each day that I work offers a new opportunity for something to be discovered. Finding enjoyment in every day is possible when you have the ability to create something which has never existed before. This is truly a miracle in the making.

It is necessary to take a close look at some of the simple things you do every day in order to make your life as joyful and special as it can be while growing to be your most perfect self. Your task is to think about how you can do these simple things with greater awareness. The key is in finding ways to pay attention to the task you are performing. You will begin to discover new experiences through attentiveness.

A good example of discovering new things through attentiveness lies in the concept of conscious eating which I discuss in Chapter Nine, The Responsibility. Very simply the idea is to pay attention to every aspect of the eating experience and in doing so find pleasure not previously recognized. Since we usually eat three times a day it only makes sense to make the most of that experience.

Consider doing this with all of the things you do throughout the day. Wear something different today just because you can and see how it makes you feel. Take an extra long shower or bath and use wonderful scents and notice how the water feels when it is very hot and very cold. In doing so you will pay closer attention to what is going on in your life, and become more aware of what is possible for you. Create new ways to exercise where you are in touch with your body and your muscles so this activity can become something of an extraordinary event, rather than a boring and painful daily chore. You might want to take Yoga or Tai Chi, or Karate or Aerobics. Maybe you would prefer to get on a bike or just walk while thinking about how your different muscles feel while contracting and releasing. Consider the attitude difference which will occur when the ordinary and mundane of your life are taken by you to a higher plane. Every day can be exciting to approach because your change of attitude will bring about a new awareness.

Consider the joy and exhilaration that will consume you when you learn to take the regimented, monotony that comprises so much of your days and nights and transform it into a unique and creative experience. What will it be like to capture all of the excitement and radiant curiosity that existed once when things were new?

"If you can walk you can dance, if you can talk you can sing."

Zimbabwe Proverb

It is true that there is nothing quite as exciting as exploring a person, place, or thing for the very first time. It is also true that as we come to know these persons, places, and things our excitement fades. It is in the knowing that our enthusiasm is muted. It is in the lack of surprise and discovery that boredom and monotony set in. However, if we make an effort to look at those persons, places, and things differently and challenge what we think we know to be true, we will constantly be discovering them for the first time. What we know to be true of them will change, and we will once again make the exhilaration of surprise and discovery part of our lives and relationships. ***Thus we have it within our power to create miracles for ourselves each and every day.***

"Be content with what you have;

Rejoice in the way things are.

When you realize there is

Nothing lacking, the whole world

belongs to you."

Lao Tzu

RECOGNIZE THE JOY OF LIFE

The Buddhist Nun Pema Chodron enlightens us with the following traditional teaching:

"Joy has to do with seeing how big, how completely unobstructed and how precious things are. Resenting what happens to you and complaining about your life are like refusing to smell the wild roses when you go for a morning walk, or like being so blind that you don't see a huge black raven when it lands in the tree that you're sitting under. We can get so caught up in our own personal pain or worries that we don't notice that the wind has come up or that somebody has put flowers on the dining room table. Resentment, bitterness, and holding a grudge prevent us from seeing and hearing and tasting and delighting."

*It is time for another exercise so get to the computer or the paper and pen and make a list of the moments of your life which have brought you joy. Write about the best day of your life in great detail.

Are you currently living in an environment where you have the ability to cultivate continuous moments of joy in your life? If not now then when?

Remember that all we have is now. There is no tomorrow, just now. We need to focus on the fact that now is wonderful, now is glorious, and <u>now</u> is our life.

Do this by allowing the moment you are currently in to completely envelop you. To do this, every time you are thinking about the past or the future while experiencing the present you must stop yourself. If you are walking along the beach and thinking about how you screwed up yesterday at the office, stop yourself, and ask the following:

What does the sand feel like under my feet? What does the sand feel like as it squishes through my toes? Do the grains get in between the crevices of my skin? Can the water touch my feet from here? Are the waves coming in or going out? Can I smell the ocean today? Can I see any shells along the waters edge? Can I see any dolphins out at sea? Can I hear the sound of the children playing or the mothers calling to them? Can I hear the whistle of the lifeguard and what does the water taste like as I swim along the waves? Think about each of your senses and focus in on what you are feeling this very moment.

This exercise can help you realize the wonderful life you have been missing. Opportunities for joy surround you. Being awake and aware helps you to see the beauty that is right there in front of you all of the time.

Look for all that is yours rather than looking for all that is missing in your life. Awaken at least once a week and watch the sunrise. Spend at least one day a week taking time to view the sunset. With these two simple activities you will begin to create a far more profound appreciation for that which is already yours. We have so much but can miss it if our focus is on what is missing rather than on what is here all around us.

Remember to say: "thank you" every day and see how this will improve your life. Before falling off to sleep, take a few moments to think about your day. Say thank you for all of the wonderful things that happened. Thank the people you work with for their time and their talents. Give thanks to those individuals who caused you pain and consider what they had to teach you.

The more you look the more you will see. The joys and pleasures of life will grow greater. This miracle of life will bring tears of joy to your eyes as the scope of what is true becomes more apparent to your heart, mind and your soul.

"Your vision will become clear only when you can look into your own heart. Who looks outside, dreams; who looks inside, awakes."

Carl Jung

"Become quiet and still

and the world will

open itself at your feet."

Franz Kafka

YOUR OWN SPACE

*Describe what area of your home will become your special place, your retreat, your sanctuary and write about what you will put in this place to make it special for you.

When we lived in a row house, I made my garden my private sanctuary. Our yard was only about twenty feet by twenty feet so I took special care to make the most of the space.

I planted flowers and set out stones and wood as edging. I even dug a hole and put in a water pump so I could hear running water as I sat in my special place. I did all of this work myself. You may be able to have it done for you, but half of the joy is that it comes from your own effort. You would lose much of the power of the place if it were not of your creation and did not have your hands in it.

I spent days working with just a pencil and paper, to lay out the design of the garden, dragging in bags of white stone and red stone. I can remember going down to the rock quarry and selecting by hand the edging rock, one piece at a time. I took the time to notice the color of each rock; some marbled and others shining like a pearl or like silver and gold.

The time I spent selecting the trees and digging the holes for the root balls, all stays with me as part of the joy of the place. Even though the work was hard, this place was mine. And in the winter when it was too cold to sit in my garden I would do my reading from the window where I could look out upon the place and still feel its power.

If you have only a corner of a room available for your creation then fill that corner with your design. My office is a small corner of a room and I have made it all mine with the simplest of items. On my computer I have placed a crystal ball and a crystal bell. On the walls I have pictures of my children and husband. I also have a prayer I have written which I say every day. And my mission statement which I read out loud each morning when I come to work.

The wall also has my vision statement on it, which simply states where I expect all of my work to lead me. I read that also every day as a constant reminder of where I am headed given that the actions which I have been taking will continue. In this way, if I decide I no longer wish to be headed in this direction; I will be reminded to change my behavior accordingly. So often goals take years to achieve and in the process what we want changes. Sometimes we are so caught up in the journey that we don't even realize it.

*Take a moment and decide what you can add to your work and private space to make them uniquely yours.

"In the middle of difficulty

lies opportunity."

Albert Einstein

THE SELF

CHAPTER SEVEN

FEAR - A BARRIER TO BE OVERCOME

LIVE YOUR LIFE WITH COURAGE

THE FACE IN THE MIRROR

SOME THOUGHTS FROM ALBERT ELLIS

THE PURE POTENTIALITY OF SELF

THE ILLUSION OF SELF ESTEEM

"To live a creative life

we must lose our fear

of being wrong."

Joseph Pearce

FEAR - A BARRIER
TO BE OVERCOME

Our goal is to improve our professional and personal lives by being more open to the possibilities around us and by eliminating the barriers and fear which impede our creativity. We are also looking to improve the way we do things to become more valuable to ourselves and to others.

Many of us spend most of our lives dealing with a very small cache of experiences. We do the same things with the same people in the same ways at the same times for the same reasons. I challenge you to stop. There is so much more of the world out there you have not yet explored just waiting for your vision once you have eliminated the fear which now stops your participation.

Pay attention to what is possible and you will live a far more enjoyable and rewarding life. You do not have to fear things you have not tried before. Rather, learn to approach new things with a childlike joy and curiosity.

Take a risk every day, and discover excitement previously missed while hiding behind your fears.

If we pay attention to the "why" of things; we will discover reasons for the fears that have prevented us from taking action in the past. We will be free and able to take action where we had previously been blocked by fear.

Sophocles said, *"Look and you will find it...What is unsought will go undetected."*

I have spent much of my life afraid of being overweight. This fear worked against my desire to be a healthy weight because I always thought in the back of my mind that I could not maintain that balance.

When I look into the reasons for this fear I go back to a time when I was no more than ten years old. Mom had taken my brother to the doctor because he was very small for his age and she wanted to see if there was something other than genetics at work. While the doctor found my brother to be in good health he said that I was the one with "the problem". He said in no uncertain terms that I was "fat". Twenty-one pounds overweight to be exact. At a very young age I began to take the diet pills this doctor had prescribed and believed I had no power over my own body.

Finally after many years of yo-yo dieting I managed to understand that the problem was in my mind and not in my stomach. I realized that until I truly believed I could maintain a healthy weight all of the diets in the world would not work. By telling myself I have the ability to be a normal weight through exercise and healthy eating and believing that from the bottom of my heart, I have found that healthy balance.

The key to this change of mind and body was to identify what negative thought had been influencing my behavior and decide what I needed to say to myself to wipe out that negative thought. By telling myself I had the power to be in charge of my body, I changed the negative influence into a positive one and began to loose my fear. With the fear eliminated I could move ahead to becoming who I was supposed to be before experiencing the negative influence of the diet doctor.

* Make a list the people who have influenced you negatively and the reason why they have caused you problems. Now write a positive message to eliminate the harmful influence and read your positive words every day. You will soon believe these new thoughts just as you chose to believe the negative ones.

We often don't take action because we are afraid of failure. A reason for our fear can be these negative thoughts which have been with us for years. Remove the harmful influence and replace it with a positive influence and you can eliminate the fear.

When working through fears and making decisions to take actions you were afraid of in the past, it is helpful to work on this exercise as a means of getting over initial fears. The simple act of preparation will help to get fear under control by realizing that you have the power to make the task work properly. Planning will give you the self-confidence you may have been missing due to lack of sufficient thought about the subject.

I learned this simple process from one for my first managers, Carmine. He taught me how to write an annual, quarterly, and monthly plan and a contingency plan just in case the original failed. I am forever grateful to him for teaching me this process as it released me from useless fears of failure and inadequacy.

*What is your objective and how will you achieve it?

What will you need to succeed and how will you utilize those resources? What is your time frame?

Make a list of everything that could possibly go wrong.

Make a list of all of the ways to prevent failure.

Who is responsible for creating success?

If everything goes wrong what is your back up position?

By the time you have finished this exercise I am certain you will conclude that you are responsible for your life. You can overcome your fear of failure by investigating the down side of an issue and planning for all of the negative possibilities. By understanding the potential for failure you can plan for success.

"Aim for success, not perfection. Never give up your right to be wrong, because then you will lose the ability to learn new things and move forward with your life. Remember that fear always lurks behind perfectionism. Confronting your fears and allowing yourself the right to be human can, paradoxically, make you a far happier and more productive person."   *Dr. David M. Burns*

When the former coach of the University of Notre Dame, Lou Holts, was asked if he was nervous before every big game his answer was no. The interviewer was surprised at his answer and requested Lou to clarify it. He said there was no reason to fear failure because his team had put in the time to prepare for the worst and understood the possible pitfalls of the day and therefore there was no reason to be afraid. Where there is sufficient planning and preparation, there is no need for fear. Fear comes when we are either unprepared or we are suffering under negative influences, telling us we are unprepared or not good enough.

Does this mean we are always going to win and succeed? No. But it means we are going to try more often and have better results more frequently than before we put together a plan for success. Every time you replace the words, "no way" with the words "you bet" you open another door which will lead toward your becoming more the essence of who you were meant to be.

Facing your fears and risking failure brings you new information to make your next attempt a victory.

I'd like to share the story of one time I faced my fears and learned something powerful which has stayed with me over the years. I had been teaching for about five hours with two hours left in a statistical process control presentation when I was struck with a most frightening dilemma. I lost the sight in my left eye. Now for most people that wouldn't be as bad as it is for me but I have no vision in my right eye, so to lose the sight in the left eye during a new seminar was devastating.

When it first came over me, I was lecturing and slowly noticing I was getting into deeper and deeper trouble. Soon I understood that the only way out of this one was to fake it! The show had to go on. I couldn't leave these people without the balance of the presentation. They had all paid a lot of money for the opportunity to learn this material.

While I was talking I began to think about how I look and act when I am well. What do I look like? How do I stand? How do I smile? How do I move my hands and my arms? How do I walk? All this was going through my mind as I was lecturing and panicking at the same time.

I decided to consciously act as I did when I was well and pretend that nothing was wrong. I cannot say that this was a great experience. It was not. I was frightened beyond belief. But I can say that I learned a whole lot about just how much power the mind has over the body.

I did manage to get through the seminar and I asked several of the participants if they had noticed anything strange about me during the presentation (just to analyze the results of my acting ability). No one noticed a thing. It was business as usual. The afternoon presentation did not seem any different from the morning presentation when I was fine.

"Life is playing a violin solo in public and learning the instrument as one goes on."
Samuel Butler

So what did I learn from this experience? First, never give up! Your mind gives up far sooner than your body will so press on and forge ahead. You can easily allow fear to take over or you can stand firm and overcome your obstacles.

Secondly, I learned to, "fake it 'til you make it". We have the power to move mountains through our positive thoughts. That is why we are told to smile when we feel badly. The act of smiling helps us to physically feel better.

I am not suggesting pushing yourself if you were suffering with a dangerous illness. I am suggesting an understanding be developed between your body and your mind so that you can judge just how far you can safely push yourself. This can be accomplished by pushing through your limits while doing physical exercise and thus coming to better understand the relationship between your body and your mind.

One of the most important things to remember is that by facing your fears and dealing with them you begin to learn one of the greatest lessons of your life. *Whatever life may throw at you, you can catch it, and throw it back. Whatever the problem, you can create a solution.*

"We need to look at our lives

with a new eye.

The eye of a stranger,

to see past the history

which currently blinds us."

Picasso

LIVE YOUR LIFE
WITH COURAGE

Make choices in your life based on the knowledge that you will be given everything you need to accomplish your life's mission because that is the reason you were put on this earth.

Remember that fear only builds barriers to the ultimate performance of your life's work and creates prisons for you to escape. Working from faith rather than from fear allows you to tear down the prison bars of fear and create the life of freedom and accomplishment for which you were created.

"Life shrinks or expands in proportion to one's courage."

Anais Nin

Are there things in your life that cannot be changed? You bet there are. Have the acuity to understand that which cannot be changed and accept those things into your life as part of your inheritance. What appears to be a curse can often turn out to be a gift. So be flexible with the way you interpret life's little glitches.

I was born with a condition which caused me to be legally blind in my right eye. Because of this condition, I tilt my head to one side, as a way of compensating for the imbalance of my sight. In doing so, the otherwise crooked world now seems straight to me.

On the surface this may seem like a terrible deficiency; but the contrary is true. My head tilt has rewarded me with an uncommon ability to help others because of the way I am perceived. People who see me perceive my head tilt as interest, caring, concern and compassion. Although that also happens to be the truth; the body language speaks much more loudly than the words could. So my handicap has become a blessing. In retrospect I think if I were given the ability to have normal sight in both eyes I wouldn't want to change what has turned out to be a wonderful asset.

"Life consists not in holding good cards but in playing those you hold well."   *Josh Billings*

No matter where you are in the circle of life; know always the words of wisdom, "This too shall pass". When you remember that nothing in this world is permanent you will always keep your balance, not feeling too low when things are down and not feeling too grand when life is high. Appreciate where you are, high or low, for what it has to teach you. Learn and grow.

Our first child, Gina, was five years old when she became very ill with the chicken pox. I can remember the day she went to the hospital vividly. Michael, was four at the time, and was just getting over the illness as was half of their school which had been suffering with an epidemic for several weeks. We were not therefore, overly concerned when Gina became infected.

It was Halloween and Gina was so upset that she had to stay home. She was going to miss all of the fun of going out for candy. As if in a nightmare she began screaming that she was in a cage and couldn't get out. She screamed that there was a bee on her ice cream and demanded that I kill it. There was no ice cream, no bee, and no cage. This was all going on in Gina's mind.

At the time I was unaware of the symptoms which occur when the chicken pox virus attacks the brain. She was hallucinating. We took her to the hospital in a panic. There they told us she had to have a spinal tap. I can remember being led out of the room listening to my baby yelling at the top of her lungs as they held her down and performed the painful procedure on her little body.

Her screaming still rings in my ears. She was so afraid and there was nothing I was able to do to console her. I felt so completely helpless. Adding insult to injury was the fact that at that time parents were not permitted to stay in the hospital with their children. I had to leave her, my precious daughter, all alone, in this cold, unfamiliar place. It was made worse knowing her state of mind.

The prognoses were everything from death, to brain damage, to partial recovery. We would just have to wait to see how the virus progressed. Gina managed to survive the illness with a challenging learning disability to remind her of the experience. Gina learned to be one of the most disciplined people I have ever known as a result of this outcome. She was unable to process information the way the other children did, so she had to find new ways to do so.

Gina would work on her homework for hours when the other children were literally done in minutes. She did this from a very young age through high school, college and graduate school. She became an excellent student because she worked for hours to do what was easy for other children. This experience taught her to be tough, focused, and determined to do what she knew she could do even if others thought it impossible for a child with these learning disabilities to achieve.

The happy ending of this story is that Gina managed to graduate from the University of Notre Dame with a double major in both Japanese and Theater. She then went on to earn her Masters degree in Education from Harvard.

Our crosses may also become our saviors, so look deeply into the trials you are sent for the hidden opportunities they may be offering.

By living her life with courage Gina was able to have faith that she would overcome her difficulties and achieve her goals in spite of the barriers. She spent two years living in Japan working for local government. There she lead an organization introducing foreigners to the Japanese culture. The next two years she taught Japanese to inner city high school students in Boston. It is anybody's guess where her crosses will lead her next.

"A problem is a chance for you to do your best."

Duke Ellington

"Be content with what you have;

Rejoice in the way things are.

When you realize there is

Nothing lacking, the whole world

belongs to you."

Lao Tzu

THE FACE IN THE MIRROR

We often limit what is possible for ourselves because we think we are not good enough. We do this by looking into the mirror and saying we are too fat, too thin, too old, too wrinkled, too stupid or too ugly. We can destroy our ability to realize our purpose by telling ourselves we will never be good enough.

Our self-esteem is based upon our beliefs about ourselves. The psychologist Albert Ellis makes an enlightening statement: *"Self-esteem is to unconditionally believe you have high value and unconditionally feel love for yourself."*

No matter what happens; you have value. Your worth comes not from others, but from within.

Your value and self esteem comes from knowing who you are at the center of your being.

In the Indian culture people greet one another with the palms of their hands pressed together as if in prayer. The meaning of this greeting is to say to the other person, I recognize the divinity within you. How powerful a tradition to give this honor to each and every being you meet.

We can learn so much from greeting every individual we meet in our lives with the recognition of who they are at their very core. Try it and see what happens to the way you view the individual and the way you feel when made aware of your own inner divinity and theirs.

When you realize that who you are is a part of this entire creation and as such you are one with it's Creator, the compassion and love from where you have come will fill your being and offer complete forgiveness and loving kindness regardless of your history.

When you realize the unconditional love which is yours for the understanding, all of your fears will seem so foolish and without meaning. You will be able to follow your purpose and dream the dreams you were meant to fulfill as the divine spirit that you are.

"Loving is the greatest teacher."

Therese of Lisieux

"If you don't like

the line you've drawn

erase it."

Linda Elerby

SOME THOUGHTS
FROM ALBERT ELLIS

You get to choose how you feel. It is not something out of your control unless you allow it. You can become more powerful in every area of your life, by understanding this simple fact.

Let me begin by giving you some understanding of the concept of Rational Emotive Therapy, created by Albert Ellis. People respond differently to the same stimuli. They have different feelings, actions, thoughts, intentions and beliefs about the same events.

For example, if you are driving down the highway and someone is tailgating you, you speed up and they speed up and finally they pass you on the right. Do you get angry at this? Do you always get angry at this or sometimes do you just pull over to the right and let the turkey pass you? All right, so sometimes you get angry and other times you don't. For some of you this is a problem and for others it just really doesn't matter. Since we all don't always get angry at the same things, it follows that it isn't always the thing which is making us angry but rather something in us.

Albert Ellis talks about the ABC's of rational thinking. It is his premise that "A", is the activating event or what happened. That "B", is the belief or how you see and interpret the value of the activating event. And finally "C", is the consequence or how you react to the situation.

What he shows is that "C", your anger or consequence, does not come from the activating event but from your belief system. Your anger does not come from the driver of the car but from how you interpret the driver of the cars behavior.

Another example he uses to help to clarify this thought is: You come out in the morning and your car is on the fritz. How do most of us feel when that happens? Do you feel angry? Why are you angry? Is it because you believe your car would never break down? That belief is not valid because we know through experience, that mechanical things will eventually break down and need repair. It is our belief that the car "should" not break down that causes the anger. Not the car breaking down.

If you adjusted your belief system to reflect reality your anger would be softened or eliminated altogether. Cars do in fact break down, you can relieve your anger by preparing for the inevitable. The car will break down. Prepare to obtain a spare car. Arrange for a loner from a friend. Have a local mechanic readily accessible. Always carry canned air for the flat tire. Have jumper cables available. All of these things (and more) can be prearranged for the inevitable event of the car breaking down. By eliminating your anger and replacing it with a contingency plan, you will feel like a success rather than a failure. So you can in many circumstances plan your way out of anger by first understanding the beliefs that get you angry and then analyzing how to make a back-up plan.

I am sure that you can see how we choose to feel angry or happy or sad, or whatever other feeling we may have. It is not perpetrated upon us. It is our choice. A choice which is uniquely human. *We get to choose how we are going to feel about a particular action. It is that ability to recognize our choice, which enhances our power to live a more successful life.*

So choose to plan for success rather than to become angry over an otherwise unavoidable situation. Decide to recognize your power to choose how you are going to feel. If you are feeling perpetually angry it is probably not entirely because of something going on outside of you but because of how you are choosing to interpret the information.

A friend of mine was having one of those frustrating times in her life. After talking about all of the difficult people she had to deal with, she remarked: "What am I a jerk magnet?" The problem was not in the people but in the way she was interpreting their actions. She would say to me this person "should have" done this or this person "should have" done that. What she needed to realize was that there are no "should haves". She was placing her belief system on the action of others and with that in place she had deemed them all to be jerks. It was not that they were jerks as much as it was that they were not her. How dare this person not be me. How dare this person have different thoughts, feelings, intentions, actions, and beliefs from mine?

Think about every time you use the words "should have" and try to understand <u>there is no such thing</u> because you have no way of knowing everything that is going on in an individuals life. So to say what they should or should not be thinking, feeling, doing, or intending; is to be acting out of ignorance.

* Make a list of the feelings you experience most often and the feelings you would like to experience more often and what actions you will take to bring you from the feelings of today to the feelings of tomorrow.

"Zen teaches nothing;

it merely enables us to wake up

and become aware.

It does not teach, it points."

D.T. Suzuki

THE PURE POTENTIALITY
OF SELF

We first become aware of who we are when we realize that our ideas are different from those of our family and our community. When we choose to follow our own beliefs, rather than those of others; we are taking that first step in developing the acorn within.

Beginning to work on your inner self will take great courage. Many people avoid this their entire lives. They fear the answers they find may be in opposition to their current lifestyles.

Because it takes great strength to go on this journey of self-discovery we sometimes prepare ourselves by first changing our outside appearance prior to making inner changes. My personal approach was to begin exercising every day with weights, to reduce my weight, and to change the color of my hair.

In order to do what you want with your life and truly be who you are you must be strong-minded. You have the ability to change your environment, by following who you are at your core. When you develop this powerful ability to effect your surroundings there is little need for fear.

When we become aware of our ability to change our lives based upon what we are thinking and the actions we are taking, our choices expand. Then we may see what is really possible for us by understanding the connection between our thoughts and our reality.

"You must first be who you really are, then do what you need to do, in order to have what you want."

Margaret Young

"In the province of the mind,

what one believes to be true either is

true or becomes true.."

John Lilly

THE ILLUSION OF
SELF ESTEEM

If you feel you have little value as a human being sometimes you may allow yourself to temporarily feel better by giving another power over you. What you are doing is letting the beliefs and values of others impact how you feel about yourself. If someone tells you that you are looking particularly wonderful today you are flying high. But if you are told you look a little fat today you may find yourself dashed to the ground and feeling worthless. Why would you want to give so much power to anyone other than yourself?

Some people develop this behavior with people. Others do it with food or booze or drugs. The impact is the same in that we give up something very precious and essential: our power. We allow someone or something else to have power over us. We sometimes allow this to occur because we don't feel that we are good enough the way we are.

"The first thing I remember liking that liked me back was food."

Rhoda Morgenstern

Now that you are both awake and aware you can begin the process of change. You can start to take back the power, which can be yours alone.

I want you to take a moment of your time now and think about the following writings of Kabir:

"You know that the seed is inside the horse-chestnut tree and inside the seed there are the blossoms of the tree and the chestnuts, and the shade. So inside the human body there is the seed, and inside the seed there is the human body again...Thinkers, listen, tell me what you know of that is not inside the soul? Take a pitcher full of water and set it down on the water. Now it has water inside and water outside. We mustn't give it a name, lest silly people start talking again about the body and the soul. If you want the truth, I'll tell you the truth; Listen to the secret sound, the real sound, which is inside you..."

In an effort to become more aware of how we allow others to have power over us; I want you to begin to work on another exercise. This will take you a bit of time. Allow yourself at least thirty minutes to give some serious thought to the work.

*Begin by making a list of the times in your life when you have felt badly about yourself. Think about how you feel when you are at work and when you are at home and what may be causing some of your negativity. Now I want you to make a list of all of the things you want people to know about you and those things which you don't want people to know and the reasons why. What you may find is that the thoughts of others are influencing the way you see who you are. Understanding the power you are giving away

188

will enable you to change this behavior. You have value because of who you are at your essence, not because of the opinions of others. This process then will allow you to become more aware of who you truly are at the core of your being.

You are not who others think you are. You are genuinely who you are; beyond all illusions. You are a child of your Creator. You hold within yourself the love and compassion of your source and because of that you are beyond clinging to the judgements of others. You are exactly what you were meant to be and becoming always more of who you are intended to become. There is no need to fear. Where there is love and compassion, you can be your perfect original self. You are complete just the way you are and filled with all you need to proceed on your journey of discovery.

When you see your true worth you will demonstrate that understanding by treating yourself with love. That means disciplining your immediate desires in lieu of your long term well being. You will not over indulge in damaging eating, drinking, shopping, gambling or whatever your particular challenge happens to be. You will instead raise your standards to honor the essence of the divine creation that you are and in doing so evolve to your most fulfilled self.

THE CHOICE

CHAPTER EIGHT

COGITO ERGO SUM

CREATE YOUR REALITY AS YOU LIKE IT

IMPROVE YOURSELF

DECISIONS, DECISIONS, DECISIONS

HONOR AND RESPECT WHO YOU ARE

"Ah, but a man's reach

should exceed his grasp

or what's a heaven for?"

Robert Browning

COGITO ERGO SUM

What I think creates my reality. Nothing will move forward for me if I do not first give it a thought. When I believe that I am a fat person, then I act like a fat person and eat all of the wrong foods. I create my reality based on my belief. Because what I think becomes that which manifests itself in my life; I have the ability to talk myself into or out of what is truth for me. If I tell myself I am a fat person I will believe it and act accordingly. I can decide that I will live my life as an overweight person or I can decide to change myself because I believe I have it within my capability to do so.

Sometimes the things we say to ourselves are so terrible we would never consider saying such things to any other human being. Yet we don't give it a second thought when we drag ourselves down with our own debilitating words. *The question then becomes; "If you don't have compassion for yourself, then for whom will you have compassion?"*

To free yourself, first forgive yourself.

"There is only one success,

to be able to spend your life

in your own way and not give

others absurd maddening claims

upon it."

Christopher Morley

CREATE YOUR REALITY
AS YOU LIKE IT

Since our thoughts create our reality, it is up to us to create a wonderful reality for ourselves. If that is what you desire, then that is what you can work towards.

* Speak into a tape recorder for three minutes defining who you are. This will force you to think more deeply by analyzing what you have said, how you said it and how it made you feel. This exercise will give you additional insight into your belief system beyond the boundaries realized by our previous exercises.

Now draw a simple picture which includes the things you love. Choose the part which means the most to you. Create a plan to include more of this thing you love into your everyday life. Then select another part of the picture and begin to add it into your everyday life. Gradually you will be doing and being more of who you are intended to be.

Our next exercise deals with getting rid of the negative thoughts we deal with on a regular basis. The theory is simply if we eliminate those negative thoughts once and for all we free up our futures to be used much more productively rather than continuously wasting our time with the same negative "stuff" time and again ad infinitum.

*Get a bag and put a post-it note on the outside of it entitled, "garbage bag". Now I want you to take some serious time and write down all of the garbage, you tend to replay in your mind. Get rid of all of the negative thoughts, the things you are afraid of and the doubts you have about your abilities by throwing them into this garbage bag you have created. Put each negative thought on a separate piece of paper and toss it into the bag. Now, take the bag out to the garbage and pitch it for the final time. Another variation on the same theme is to take the bag outside with a shovel and bury the garbage; reminding you it is dead, once and for all and will never again be exhumed.

What you are doing is making a ritual for yourself to remind you every time you fall into those repetitive negative thought patterns you have grown accustomed to over the years. Once again making you more aware of the present as a tool to free yourself to be open to what is most important to your development.

"If you think you can do a thing, or think you can't do a thing; you're right."

Henry Ford

"The mode by which the

inevitable comes to pass

is through effort."

Oliver Wendell Holmes

IMPROVE YOURSELF

Acknowledging how things are right now will help you to move on to improvement.

You are the only one in this world who can solve your problems and answer your questions about who and what you are. There is no one outside of yourself who can do this. You are the answer to all of the questions you have about your life. Look within to find the wisdom, which has always been there, waiting for you to ask.

There is no person in this entire world who is able to do for you what you can do for yourself. Not your mother, not your preacher, not your therapist, no one. Only you have the power to create positive change.

When we accept what others are telling us about our lack of power we lose our abilities because we believe what they are saying as truth. Our work becomes learning to trust in the intuitive powers we were born with. Picasso says, *"It takes a long time to become young."*

Your work then is to identify the problems you are experiencing and fix them knowing you have the insight to do so. Just as in the case of an automobile; if you locate the problems and repair them you should be able to drive the car for many years. But if you ignore the problems you will probably destroy the car long before its time.

"So much is a man worth as he esteems himself."

Francois Rabelais

We exhibit a lack of self-confidence in many ways. The most obvious example is through the language we choose to use. A successful person will use the word "try" no more than once a day where as an unsuccessful person would use the word "try" eight or nine times in one day.

What is implied in the use of the word "try"? The possibility of failure is implied. *If you do not believe in your own success then who will believe in you?*

In the words of "Star War's" famous philosopher, Yoda, "Try, try, no try, DO!"

*Free yourself of constant judgment and move on with your personal improvement process. Make a list of the demands and criticisms you make of yourself both at work and at home and reflect on the results. Learn from the exercise to avoid useless self-imposed pressures and move on to the future, free from worthless old habits.

Eliminating unnecessary work and negative feelings will free you to spend your time on those things which are most important to your improvement process.

"Pain makes man think.

Thought makes man wise.

Wisdom makes life endurable."

John Patrick

DECISIONS, DECISIONS, DECISIONS

Because energy manifests into matter through your thoughts, you have the power of creation within yourself. Since the choices you make do in fact create your life; it is a good idea to understand where those choices originate.

Do we make our choices based on fear of all that we don't have or do we make our choices based on knowing that we have everything we need to live our purpose right now? Do our choices come from a place of deprivation or from a place of bounty? When you answer this question consider the different life you would have if your choices come from a place of confidence rather than a place of fear.

Start with a decision you need to make and consider the alternatives. My favorite approach is the Benjamin Franklin technique: write the positive and negative possibilities created by each proposed action. In doing so you will be able to analyze if your decision is based upon fear or abundance. Narrow your choice to a couple of options and think of them as different foods. One of your options can be meat and the other may be potatoes. Your job is to put each of the options into your mouth and chew it, swallow it, and digest it. If you feel comfortable after you have eaten it; go ahead and move in that direction. If you feel sick to your stomach, it is not the correct decision for you.

Remember you were born with the intuition needed to make the best decisions for yourself. Only you can make the decisions, which will create the life you were born to live. Listen, be kind to yourself, love yourself!

"Decide what you want, decide what you are willing to exchange for it. Establish your priorities and go to work."

H.L.Hunt

No more excuses, no more blame, no more guilt. The time has come to take responsibility for your own fate. You will have the ability to make proper decisions for yourself when you give yourself the gift of absolute love.

You know what happens when another gives you unrestricted love? All of the barriers come down because this person will love you no matter what, so no need to be afraid. Imagine the power of giving that gift of unconditional love to yourself.

Decisions based on love, rather than on fear will be decisions which will nurture rather than ignore your acorn within.

"Listen to the exhortation of the dawn! For it is life, the very life of life... in its brief course lie all the verities and realities of your existence; the bliss of growth, the glory of action, the splendor of beauty: for yesterday is but a dream, and tomorrow is only a vision, but today well lived makes every yesterday a dream of happiness, and every tomorrow a vision of hope. Look well therefore to this day! Such is the salutation of the dawn!"

Author Unknown

from the Sanskrit

HONOR AND RESPECT
WHO YOU ARE

Jesus said, *"You are the light of the world."*

Buddha said, *"Be lamps unto yourselves; be your own confidence. Hold to the truth within yourselves as the only truth."*

In the Hebrew tradition God said, *"Behold, I will put my law within them, and I will write upon their hearts, and I will be their God, and they will be my people."*

Understanding the truth about who we are will set our course and our path and forecast our destination. How we see ourselves in this world, will cause us to make choices about who we love and what we do with our lives.

If we see ourselves as having value we make positive decisions. If we see ourselves as not being worthy we make negative decisions. Freedom comes from recognizing our own light within. Our challenge is to search for that light.

I spent so many years of my life hiding the true me from my family and friends alike. No one knew who I really was. No one understood how I felt about the work I was doing or the work I needed to do. I thought that if I conformed to what they wanted me to be, they would love me and I

wouldn't rock the boat. I pretended to be someone I was not for the sake of pleasing others for many years. The only person I really needed to please, to put things right, was my own true self. By finally taking the time to identify and share my true feelings with my family, they were able to see who I really was. They loved the real me, rather than the image of me I had created for them.

By taking these actions my behavior is finally in complete alignment with who I am. I am at peace and at ease with who that person is for the first time in my life.

By respecting who I am at the center of my being, I can begin to understand what fulfillment means to me because I am working in congruence with my thoughts, feelings and desires. I now can find my true value within myself rather than relying on the acceptance of others to give me value. Think of the power of depending on your intuition and the information you are receiving from your inner self to give you the correct answers. You make decisions based on what is truth for you rather than relying on what is true for others.

I now find myself on the most extraordinary journey of my lifetime. I am thrilled to meet every new day for what it will teach me and I am constantly challenged by new possibilities and opportunities which arise before me. I find that as long as I am moving forward and discovering something new, even though I am far from where I want to be; I am happy with myself and my performance regardless of what others think.

Embrace your beliefs and your thoughts and let your loved ones know about them, because they are not only your present but the source of your future as well.

I can remember the experience of pure joy and freedom when I told my family what I wanted to do with the rest of my life. Finally I found the courage to tell them I wanted to drop all corporate work and write this book and spend all of my time doing personal development seminars. I knew that would be hard for them to accept because there was much more risk without the corporate business. But this was where I knew I had to be.

I now have time to devote to what is important to fulfilling my purpose. Besides freeing up my mind, telling my loved ones the truth has eliminated daily stomach pain I had suffered with for years while trying to hide my true self.

Living your life in congruence with who you are opens the doors to a peace unlike anything you could possibly imagine.

THE RESPONSIBILITY

<u>CHAPTER NINE</u>

FREEDOM, HAPPINESS AND HEALTH

PLAN FOR A HEALTHY LIFESTYLE

DESIGNING YOUR CUSTOM DIET

EATING LESS AND ENJOYING IT MORE

YOUR DAILY BURN

GOOD WORK ENCOURAGES GOOD HEALTH

"Somewhere deep down we know

that in the final analysis we do decide

things and that even our decisions to

let someone else decide are really our

decisions, however pusillanimous."

Harvey Cox

FREEDOM, HAPPINESS,
AND HEALTH

"Be not a prisoner of yourself or your work to achieve freedom and health", Kahlil Gibran said in his book, <u>The Prophet.</u>

As we have discussed, we are free to make our own choices and decisions. We are free to choose how we will respond to different stimuli. No one can make us think anything we do not want to think.

Since you have the freedom to choose, ask yourself if you have chosen to create a healthy lifestyle for yourself. If you are currently forced by outside constraints to live without the proper food and exercise on a daily basis, then it is time for you to reassess your options. ***Living without the proper food and exercise will create a barrier, which will inhibit your growth as a human being.***

Sometimes it is our own desires which put us in situations where we are unable to obtain the proper food and exercise. Ask yourself if this is the case and re-evaluate your decision making process.

Work to understand the reason you are mistreating your body. Learn to listen to your heart and realize that if you value yourself you will treat your body with honor and not neglect.

Back in the early eighties while working in Manhattan I chose to create my own illness. I ate nothing but fast food. I smoked two packs of cigarettes a day. I did no exercise, and I worked in a high stress environment. I did all of these things by my own choice. The net result was that I gained lots of weight, experienced chest pain, dizziness, tingling of the feet and hands and finally thought I was going to die if I didn't change my behavior. After sinking to the bottom of the barrel, I finally chose life over death by changing my entire lifestyle.

"With your talents and industry with science, and that steadfast honesty which eternally pursues right, regardless of consequences, you may promise yourself everything but health, without which there is no happiness. An attention to health then should take the place of every other object. The time necessary to secure this by active exercises, should be devoted to it in preference to every other pursuit." Jefferson said this in 1787, and his words are as true today as they were then.

Consider how you might incorporate this thought into your life. Creating a healthy lifestyle for yourself should probably be on the top of your list, if you are to become the person you are meant to be.

Your body is constantly changing, and not necessarily for the better. That is, unless you take action toward that end. As we age we automatically begin to lose muscle tone. Year after year the loss of muscle will continue unless we do something about it. Loss of muscle contributes to your body gaining fat and the relationship between lean body mass to fat changes until you are putting yourself at risk of heart disease, diabetes, and cancer. Because muscle burns more calories than fat our goal needs to be to increase muscle mass as a means of controlling our weight as we age.

At the turn of the century in 1900 the average life expectancy was forty-seven years old. Today, if you live relatively healthy into your fifties, you can expect to live into your eighties or nineties. Choosing a healthy lifestyle will increase your chances of being productive, well into your golden years.

"Our body is precious,

it is our vehicle for awakening;

treat it with care."

Buddha

PLAN FOR A
HEALTHY LIFESTYLE

Let us take a moment and create the foundations of a healthy lifestyle for ourselves. Write out the answers to the following questions to help you to define all of the steps needed for you to change your current behavior.

*What would a healthy lifestyle look like for you?

How would you go about achieving that lifestyle? What steps would you need to take?

Could you do it in concert with your existing environment or would you have to recreate your environment in order to make good health a priority? How would you restructure your environment?

Since our body is a precious vehicle for awakening, we need to treat it with care by eating slowly and listening to what it has to tell us. Remember to let your stomach tell you when to stop eating as opposed to letting your eyes and tongue tell you when to push away from the table.

*Ask yourself how much exercise do you get every day?

How much weight bearing exercise? How much aerobic exercise and how much stretching?

If you are not now spending a sufficient amount of time keeping your body healthy, then you want to consult a physician for input on your particular needs.

To get and keep fit the average person would want to consider daily exercise, if possible. The complete daily regimen should consist of at least ten minutes of stretching, fifteen minutes of doing weight bearing exercises and thirty minutes of aerobic exercise. The key to the success of any program, of course, is consistency.

If your current demands do not allow you to spend an hour a day caring for your body then it is time to re-evaluate them. If however, you have the ability to get up just thirty minutes earlier and go to sleep just thirty minutes later, and still obtain your required amount of sleep, then you don't have to make any other adjustments to incorporate your new health maintenance program.

If you find that time is a barrier to beginning a healthy lifestyle; you can do a simple time study as we suggested earlier in the book. This will identify how you can incorporate a permanent change into your limited schedule.

You must approach this in a very disciplined and logical fashion. You will not find the time to exercise by accident. You must understand how you are spending your time now, see how you can eliminate less valuable tasks, and replace them with revitalizing workouts.

As I have said, consistency is the only way to get results. To become consistent in your workouts you might want to consider cross-training. All that means quite simply is that you train in different disciplines. One day your aerobic work might be in swimming and the next in tennis, the following in bicycling and the next in walking through the park. Notice how this can sound less difficult to deal with than thirty minutes a day on a treadmill.

The point is to do what you enjoy, to make the training as much fun as it can possibly be for you. If you hate what you are doing, you will never become consistent and the value will be lost.

Some people love the structure of going to a gym every day while others prefer training in their own homes. Videos are wonderful tools to help you with your workouts. They can teach you how to balance your work and help to keep you motivated in a very inexpensive way. Weight training can also be done at home with the purchase of some inexpensive free weights and a video. I recommend the Cory Everson tapes for basic instructional information.

"Men are born soft and supple; dead, they are stiff and hard. Plants are born tender and pliant; dead, they are brittle and dry. Thus whoever is stiff and inflexible is a disciple of death. Whoever is soft and yielding is a disciple of life. The hard and the stiff will be broken, the soft and supple will prevail."   *Kahlil Gibran.*

Both mental and physical stiffness can be worked through to become flexible. If you have become stiff over the years know that you are not alone and that many share your challenge.   Understand however, that you have it within yourself to reverse the process through consistent exercise.

We develop patterns of lifestyles with the passing of many years. We feel comfortable with the way we do things and therefore it is possible that when you try to change your lifestyle to include daily exercise, you may not succeed at first. Relax, there's no rush. Take your time and find what will work best for you.

This will probably mean you will have to change the way you are currently doing things. As the Buddha teaches, "Learn to let go, that is the key to happiness." Let go of the way you used to do things for a new and better way, a life affirming way, a way of the spirit and the soul, of the mind and of the body.

Consider what Buddha meant when he told us that, *"Simplicity brings more happiness than complexity."* Consider that to add a new way of living which includes healthy eating and consistent daily exercise to your life may mean simplifying how you are now spending your time.   Know that making your life simpler will open up new vistas of joy for you to embrace. You will begin to see things which have been there all of the time, but in your complex life you have been missing much of their beauty.   Eliminate complexity and replace it with simplicity. Good eating and consistent exercise, are two necessary components to a healthy lifestyle.

"For the very true beginning of wisdom is the desire of discipline; and the care of discipline is love."   *Wisdom of Solomon*

215

"Knowing others is intelligence;
knowing yourself is true wisdom.
Mastering others is strength;
mastering yourself is true power.
If you realize that you have enough, you
are truly rich."

Lao-Tzu

DESIGNING YOUR
CUSTOM DIET

The American Cancer Society reports that thirty five percent of all cancer deaths are attributable to diet. Understanding once again that we are <u>less victim</u> than we had previously thought, encourages us to take an active part in the health of our bodies.

Let's take a look at your diet and see what you can do about improving it. Once again it is important to take out a piece of paper or turn on the computer and begin to write out the answers to the following questions:

*What does your average meal look like? What are the contents of your breakfast, lunch, dinner and the snacks you usually consume?

It is a wonderful and powerful exercise to keep track of what you are actually eating for one week. When you are keeping account of your food intake also remember to write down not only what you are eating but also when you are eating. This will give you some insight about your current food demands.

An additional suggestion in creating an improved food program is to include how you were feeling when you were eating. This little trick will illuminate possible emotional eating as opposed to eating due to hunger. Understanding the reason you are eating is a first step to correcting damaging behavior. If you are currently eating fried foods; eliminate them from your diet to cut as much wasted fat and wasted calories as possible. Your body only requires small amounts of protein so be cautious with the number of ounces of protein you allow yourself per day in the form of meat, chicken and fish. Keep eggs to about three a week. Ask your doctor for specific advice for your body's needs. Look at the amount of dairy you are consuming and try to use skim milk and low fat cheeses in your diet rather than fat laden dairy products. Grains are a great source of fiber and vitamins and you should incorporate the proper amount daily into your diet. Use the United States Food and Drug Administration Pyramid chart to decide on the amount from each food group which will best serve the needs of your mind and body.

The pyramid suggests six to eleven servings of bread, two to four servings of fruit, three to five servings of vegetables, two to three servings of meat, two to three servings of milk, and fats and sweets to be used sparingly.

Author and physician Dr. Andrew Weil suggests specific foods and additives in his book, Eight Weeks To Optimum Health, which I strongly recommend. I am including several of his ideas for your convenience.

Coffee irritates the stomach. Give it up or replace it with cancer fighting green tea. It has caffeine in it so you will be able to awaken as with the coffee. What I have done is limit myself to one cup of coffee and one cup of green tea and that seems to be the best I am able to do for the moment. I will however continue to try to eliminate that one cup of coffee completely. My prior coffee intake had been as high as five cups a day, so there is always hope.

Replace your oils with olive oil a monounsaturated fat, which is much better than polyunsaturated or saturated fat.

Eat forty grams of fiber a day. (Twice the current American average.) It is also a good idea to replace two meat meals a week with a soy product. Soy is currently being tested for its ability to fight heart disease and cancer, as well as to protect bone density and minimize hot flashes. This could be an alternative to hormone replacement therapy. I am currently using this coarse of treatment and waiting for the final results on the overall benefits of soy.

Another suggestion to improve your health is to replace two days of meat eating with eating fish.

Adding garlic to your diet is a good idea. It seems to be wonderful for the cardiovascular system, for its anti cancer work, for its antibiotic attributes, its ability to lower blood pressure and cholesterol, and for stimulating the immune system.

The American Cancer Society suggests that we use meat as a side dish rather than as the main part of the meal. Have broccoli twice a week and eat it only slightly cooked for optimal benefit. Do the same with cooked greens like collards, kale, chard, beet or mustard greens.

Make fresh ginger a part of your new healthy diet and use it by grating it into your tea or over your foods. Its also wonderful for stomach upsets when boiled in water.

Dr. Weil suggests taking a number of diet supplements of which I'll give a brief synopsis. I strongly suggest that you read his book and talk with your doctor about the optimal dosages right for you. He talks about taking additional vitamin C, vitamin E, Beta Carotene with related compounds Lycopene, Selenium, and others.

What time do you stop eating in the evening? Try to stop eating two to three hours before you go to bed and by doing so you will improve the quality of your food intake and your digestion as well.

I have personally struggled with maintaining my weight for most of my life. It has only been during these past ten years while I have been paying attention to who I am and what is important to me that I have finally found the magic of balance in my life and how that balance impacts my ability to control my weight. Much to my initial surprise weight management is less about control and more about a natural process of creating equilibrium in the body. I can help create that interior balance by the kind words I choose to give to myself about what is possible for me. I also achieve balance by accepting the present state of my body and mind and understanding the power of that union.

"To master the pride of defiant selfhood, that in truth is the highest bliss. The sovereign will is found where a man conquers himself, declining to be a prisoner either of himself or of his worldly tasks."

Buddha

EATING LESS AND
ENJOYING IT MORE

The great trick to taking in fewer calories and enjoying those fewer calories more than you were enjoying greater amounts of food is called "conscious eating". This idea comes to us from the Buddhists. While staying at a Buddhist temple in Koiya San, Japan; I had the opportunity to learn how the monks are able to eat a strictly vegetarian diet and be satisfied with what seemed to me to be vastly less food than the American male normally consumes.

Part of the Buddhist philosophy entails living in the present rather than in the future or the past. When you are applying this principle to food, living in the present means that you eat in a different "way".

"He who binds to himself a joy does the winged life destroy; but he who kisses the joy as it flies lives in eternity's sun rise."

William Blake

At the temple, eating is done in silence. There is no talking, no music, no television, nothing to distract you from what you are doing. Instead of your mind being involved in other activities while you thoughtlessly shovel volumes of food into your mouth, you are mindful of every morsel of food you consume. This is conscious eating.

Something I noticed about what the monks ate which was very different, was the large variety of foods they consume during one meal. Although the portions were very small, the tastes, smells, textures and colors of each of the foods were all quite different.

Another noticeable difference was the size of their dishes. There was never a large dish used, rather there were many small separate dishes each prepared for one person to consume without the option of additional food.

It should also be noted that the Japanese do not drink a beverage with their meals. The only beverage they have is served after the meal is finished and it is a cup of hot green tea.

Think about what would happen if you did not have a beverage alongside of your meal to wash down your food. If you try it just one time you will find the process of eating takes much longer when not accompanied by a liquid.

You will also notice that you are far more aware of the taste of the foods you are eating if you are not continuously diluting them with a beverage.

Let me take you back to the beginning of your meal and how you would approach it. After you have prepared this well-balanced meal of great variety and small portions you will sit and look at your meal with no distractions. Observe and enjoy the look of the food. Light a candle even if you are eating alone. Take a moment to appreciate the colors and the way the light hits the food. Breathe in the aroma. Find pleasures in the sight and smell of your meal. You must take the time to do this. You will find that food can become a much more sensual pleasure while also being far more healthy for you.

"One eats in holiness and the table become an altar."

Martin Buber

After you have enjoyed the initial step to conscious eating; select one food to taste. Watch how you pick up the food with your fork. Take only a small amount of food at a time and begin to fully appreciate every mouthful. If you want to train yourself on the proper amount of food to give yourself in each bite, try using chopsticks for about a week. This new skill will help to slow down your intake and give yourself more appropriate amounts of food.

When you get this small piece of food up to your mouth, look at it and enjoy the aromas. Think about what it feels like when you take the food into your mouth and begin to chew it. Really appreciate the textures of the food. Think about the flavors you are enjoying.

"If only we could pull out our brain and use only our eyes", Picasso reminds us to slow down. We are reminded to use

our eyes to see that which is new every time and not permit our brain to speed ahead in many different directions and dilute the wonderful pleasures our eyes can afford us as we begin the process of eating a meal.

You will find as you practice conscious eating that you are far more satisfied with far less food. There are basically two reasons for this. First, it takes twenty minutes for your brain to receive the message from your stomach that you have had enough food. This methodology slows your intake to the point where your brain has sufficient time to send the satisfaction message before you have over consumed. The second reason you are more satisfied with less food is because you have made yourself aware of the pleasures you have previously ignored.

Thus, you will find you can eat less with more pleasure rather than feeling deprived of greater amounts of food which can be a formula for disaster in the traditional western style of "dieting".

"Everything flows,

nothing remains"

Herakleitos

YOUR DAILY BURN

How many calories does your body burn daily? Part of understanding how to manage your weight is knowing how many calories you can consume without gaining. If your goal is to loose weight, you can see how many calories you need to cut in order to begin the loosing process. If your desire is to gain weight you can also understand what needs to be added to your diet to increase your size.

Use the following formula to determine your resting metabolic rate:

*FOR MEN

WEIGHT in pounds multiplied by 6.2 = X

HEIGHT in inches multiplied by 12.7 = Y

X+Y+655=Z

YOUR AGE multiplied by 6.8 = A

Z-A= B (YOUR RESTING METABOLIC RATE)

FOR WOMEN

WEIGHT in pounds multiplied by 4.3 = X

HEIGHT in inches multiplied by 4.3 = Y

X+Y+655=Z

YOUR AGE multiplied by 4.7 = A

Z-A= B (YOUR RESTING METABOLIC RATE)

This formula will tell you how many calories you need to maintain your weight with your present activity level. Apply the following formula to the number you got for your resting metabolic rate:

B=YOUR RESTING METABOLIC RATE

B multiplied by 1.8 = C (YOUR METABOLIC RATE IF YOU ARE AN ATHLETE)

B multiplied by 1.4 = D (YOUR METABOLIC RATE IF YOU DO AN AVERAGE AMOUNT OF EXERCISE)

B multiplied by 1.2 = E (YOUR METABOLIC RATE IF YOU ARE A COUCH POTATO)

If your goal is to loose weight then determine how many calories you will be able to take in to maintain your new desired weight. To lose weight, eat 20% fewer calories than your goal weight requires you to eat.

What percent of fat do you have in your diet today? To maintain a healthy balance try not to exceed 30% of your diet in fat. Today we are fortunate to have fat content listed on most of the foods we buy in the supermarket. Read the labels and keep track of how much fat you are consuming to stay "heart healthy".

We need to understand the enormous value of not being a slave to our own desires. To observe moderation in all things is a powerful thought to live by as a means of true self-mastery.

"Love is the magician, the enchanter that changes worthless things to joy…

It is the perfume of that wondrous flower, the heart, and without that sacred passion, that divine swoon, we are less than beasts, but with it, earth is heaven, and we are Gods."

Robert Ingersoll

GOOD WORK ENCOURAGES
GOOD HEALTH

Do you love your work?

To truly love your work, your efforts must benefit both yourself and someone else. Since we spend so much of our time doing our work; it is essential to find the goodness and passion in the work that we do, even in the simplest of tasks.

Since most of us will probably do simple things, rather than do great things; it is our job to figure out how to do simple things greatly.

Let's do an exercise now to help us with the process of making an ordinary job extraordinary.

*Write down the names of five people you know and the work they do. Now jot down thoughts on how these people can improve the "way" they do their jobs to benefit both themselves and others.

Let me give you an example.

One of my managers had an employee named Doris. She had a rather ordinary job ringing up sales and selling film and processing services. Doris added to her work a sense of humor, which was a gift to every customer, fortunate enough to do business with her. Doris always had a new joke for her customers. She made them laugh and they tried to do the same for Doris. She lifted the spirits of person after person and they in turn lifted her spirits and perhaps even the people they touched throughout the day, all thanks to the efforts of the sales clerk doing her job in an extraordinary way.

"At the height of laughter, the universe is flung into a kaleidoscope of new possibilities."

Jean Huston

What is the value of your work if you lift the spirits of other human beings by the "way" you work? Should the value of your work be determined by how much money you make or should we determine the value based on a higher standard?

*Write about the way you work and how you can move it out of the ordinary to a totally different plane of activity. We are talking about making our work spiritually rewarding - supporting body, mind, and soul.

I have created seminars designed to lift the spirits of the participants by recognizing their unique characteristics and abilities. This is accomplished using various techniques of reward, recognition, laughter, love, team efforts, individual efforts, and lots of surprises. This method not only makes

232

the learning more enjoyable for the students but for me as well. Thus my work can be both spiritually and financially rewarding.

I am helping to create good health for both myself and my audience by lifting our spirits. When we laugh and we are happy, it causes chemicals to be released in our bodies which, in turn, produce a feeling of wellness. Good health and good work go hand and hand.

"Gladness of the heart is the life of a man, and the joyfulness of a man prolongeth his days."

Ecclesiasticus 30:20

THE PEACE

CHAPTER TEN

MEDITATION MADE SIMPLE

THE POWER OF YOUR BREATH

EAST MEETS WEST - ZAZEN

Who is it that can make the muddy

water clear?

No one, but if left to stand,

it will gradually become

clear of itself."

The Tao Te Ching

MEDITATION MADE SIMPLE

Meditation does not have to be some deep and mystical experience reserved only for the yogis of the east. Quite the contrary, meditation should be, and is, something simple and accessible to everyone.

My grandmother used to call it her quiet time. She would spend just ten minutes a day sitting alone in the midst of six children and listen to the silence within. My mother also practiced this simple form of meditation every day. She said she needed this time for herself. She would sit on our red and white loveseat and close her eyes and enjoy the peace. My mother was by far the gentlest person I have ever known. I can remember the priest who used to come to visit Mom when she was preparing to die saying the same thing about her. He had never in his life known such a gentle human being. It requires some effort for most of us to get to that place of peace and harmony and gentle kindness. But meditation can help.

Some examples of ways to meditate include simple breathing exercises that calm the body and quiet the mind.

The repetition of a mantra or a word to help to quiet the mind also works well for some people. Visualizing a special place and allowing your mind to transport you where you are naturally quiet and calm is another approach.

There are numerous ways to meditate. You should choose the one which fits best with who you are. I will explain several examples to you and I encourage you to read further on the topic as you become more adept at the simpler techniques and find you are ready for more elaborate approaches.

I will give you a simple example of a breathing meditation but don't let it inhibit your imagination.

*Sit in a room where you can have ten to twenty minutes of silence. Sitting on the floor with your back straight and your legs crossed is a comfortable way to begin. Place your hands on your legs palms up. Look downward and empty your mind by counting your breaths. Do not force your breath, just count them in and out. Breathe in through your nose and out through your mouth. Think about nothing but your breaths.

When you first begin the process of meditation you will find your mind flying everywhere. Just let it be. Return to counting your breaths. With practice you will manage to come to a place where you are free from inner distraction. Your thoughts will leave you to rest and you will simply be. You will find joy in these moments of peace.

*Your exercise now is to actually work through this first meditative process and then take several minutes to write about how it made you feel and what thoughts entered and left your mind.

The Dalai Lama says this, *"During the actual practice of meditation, recall the subject of your meditation, as you begin each new day, you should generate a strong motivation, thinking, from now until I die I will try my best to be useful, to be beneficial to other people. At least I will not harm them. I will try to do that until I die, and at least that is what I will do today. Then before you close your eyes at night, you should think back on how you spent your day. If you find that your conduct was useful and beneficial you can rejoice and make a further determination to spend the rest of your life this way. If you find that you behaved negatively, that you bullied someone or said something nasty or harmful, you must openly admit it. Confess your mistake and make a determination not to do the same again. If you do not pay attention to this kind of objective, but simply go on leading the same old way of life, you will make no progress."*

"We must learn to be still

in the midst of activity

and to be vibrantly alive

in repose."

Gandhi

THE POWER OF YOUR BREATH

Breathing exercises are a basic form of relaxation and meditation and are a way to harmonize body, mind and spirit. Dr. Weil suggests the following daily routine for breathing exercises, (which I swear by) as a tool to better health:

Breath exercises. In the morning he suggests doing a stimulating breath, a relaxing breath, breath observation, and reversal of inhale and exhale. At bedtime he suggests letting yourself be breathed and the relaxing breath.

With stimulating breath you are energized. You can use this in the middle of the afternoon when you are feeling rather sluggish. To begin the process first inhale and exhale quickly, three times per second, at the same level on each so you can hear the breath. Start with fifteen seconds and gradually build up to a full minute. This exercise, will pick up your spirits as you feel the energy increased in your body.

To practice relaxing breathing, begin with the tongue lightly touching the roof of your mouth behind your teeth.

Exhale loudly and inhale to the count of four and hold to the count of seven. Next exhale to the count of eight and begin the process again for a total of eight repetitions two times a day. Empty your mind of clutter and listen to what the universe has to tell you.

Breath observation means you become aware of and watch your breath. This exercise is calming and should be done for five minutes.

Letting yourself be breathed, deals with allowing yourself to feel as though the breath of the universe were being breathed into your body and you in return were breathing your breath into the whole of the universe. Do this ten times once a day.

Visualization can help make this exercise more powerful to you as an individual. You have to find the picture which works best for you. I visualize the picture of God breathing life into Adam by Michelangelo and Adam in return exhaling his breath back into his Creator. That, for me, is a wonderful visual on which to focus as I inhale and exhale and feel the great compassion of the life giving force coming into my body and the wisdom of the world being returned to the great life giving force.

At times I repeat on the inhale, **"Fill me with love and compassion and forgiveness."** On the exhale I repeat, **"Empty me of all of the fear and anger and hatred and ignorance so I can be filled with (inhale) the power of unconditional love, compassion and forgiveness and** (exhale) observe as the barriers I have created for myself built of fear and anger and ignorance come tumbling down. Leaving open wide the space to be filled with pure (inhale) love and compassion and forgiveness and truth."

This is a technique works well for me. Be free to develop your own meditation and let it grow and change based on your own personal needs.

I have felt the revelation of the most important knowledge I have been given to date during these moments of quiet and listening within. I have come to feel the power of unconditional love and forgiveness and the freedom of understanding that a world of unlimited possibilities has been opened before me.

Where there is unconditional love and freedom from fear; there is freedom beyond all measure. When you realize there is nothing to be desired because at your essence you have everything you need to become the person you were destined to become; light floods your soul and tears cleanse your eyes. You see for the very first time what is the truth for you and are awed by its beauty.

"Sell your cleverness

and buy

bewilderment."

Rumi

EAST MEETS WEST – ZAZEN

The meaning of Zazen comes first from the Chinese, "za" which means to sit. The word "Zen" comes from the Sanskrit term meaning to contemplate. So the term Zazen means to contemplate while sitting.

This form of meditation will help you to find your way to a deeper understanding of your life. If you consider some of the decisions you have made in your life you may find that many of them were made simply because others were making similar decisions at that particular time. When I was young couples would marry in their late teens to early twenties as opposed to today when the average age for marriage is in the late twenties. So perhaps part of the reason many people made the decision to marry in their early twenties was because everyone else was doing that at that time.

To quote the uniquely gifted Yogi Berra, *"Don't follow the crowd, nobody is going there any more, it's too crowded."* Following the crowd might not be the best way to make decisions and the use of Zazen will help you to choose the decisions which are best for you.

To stop and think and find a clear mind, this is Zazen. In finding a clear mind you will be better prepared to make decisions based on your individual needs rather than on what others are doing.

"I have found power in the mysteries of thought."

Euripides

To begin find a quiet place, wear loose clothing and sit legs crossed on a comfortable pillow.

First you must find the perfect position for your body and then you must find the perfect position for your mind. To do this you must quiet your mind by thinking of nothing.

The eyes can be kept slightly open but may also be closed. The ears should be in alignment with the shoulders and the nose in alignment with the navel.

Find the "soku", which is the quiet and continuous breath. Take long deep breathes where your abdomen pulls in as you exhale. When you have pushed out all of the air, you will inhale and expand your abdomen until it is filled with air. Count your breaths to keep focused.

Zazen is well worth the effort because with time; you will find a place of great peace and joy at the very center of your being. Here you will be able to find freedom from the rush of your daily life and the chaos of your frantically busy mind.

THE JOY

CHAPTER ELEVEN

BUT ARE YOU REALLY HAPPY?

BALANCE YOUR LIFE WITH WHO YOU LOVE

MAKE JUST ONE SOMEONE SMILE

ACTIVE PHILOSOPHY VS. PASSIVE PHILOSOPHY

LET GO OF RESENTMENT

ALL MAJOR RELIGIONS

GOOD TO KNOW YOU ARE NOT ALONE

246

"If we could see the miracle

of a single flower clearly…

our whole life would change."

Albert Einstein

BUT ARE YOU REALLY HAPPY?

Let us contemplate a basic truth on which much of this book is based: *All men and women desire happiness*. It doesn't take much to observe that all work toward that end and it is natural as the sun rising every morning and setting every evening. It just is the way we act. We are programmed by our nature to pursue happiness by fulfilling our desires as much as is humanly possible.

*Take a moment and consider all of your fears and problems. Now consider all of your wants and needs, and desires. When you have taken the time to do this you will notice that all of these emotions stem from your very fundamental drive to seek happiness.

Without this constant search for happiness there would be no fear and no anxiety. We would accept our fate, whether it were either toward The Good or away from The Good. In each of us there is a constant pull toward happiness. We search for it because it is the attainment of all of our desires toward goodness, which is the ultimate attainment and the ultimate end. Since we are drawn toward this good as a part of who we are, our basic source of being is goodness and the ultimate good forces us onward and upward.

The philosopher St. Augustine says, *"Happy is he who has all that he wills and wills nothing evil."* And so happiness occurs when all of the obstacles are removed from our path to obtain that which we desire. When all of our desires are satisfied, we are at peace and happy. Thus we cannot be perfectly happy as long as there remains some object of desire to pursue. And so our happiness can never be perfect and complete; but can be a journey toward the ultimate good.

There is so much we do not know in this life. We can only move ahead with the knowledge we do have and do our best to work toward the good of all. A very beautiful poem by San Juan De La Cruz speaks to the issue of finding happiness in such a beautiful way I thought that sharing it with you might create new insights:

"I came into the unknown and stayed there unknowing, rising beyond all science.

I did not know the door but when I found the way, unknowing where I was, I learned enormous things, but what I felt I cannot say, for I remained unknowing, rising beyond all science.

It was the perfect realm of holiness and peace. In deepest solitude I found the narrow way; a secret giving such release that I was stunned and stammering, rising beyond all science.

I was so far inside, so dazed and far away my senses were released from feelings of my own. My mind had found a surer way; a knowledge by unknowing, rising beyond all science.

And he who does arrive collapses as in sleep, for all he knew before now seems a lowly thing, and so his knowledge grows so deep that he remains unknowing, rising beyond all science."

Although we all speak of happiness as though we knew what would satisfy that deep desire within each of us; I think what we are really after is an experience with the Divine. We buy new homes, clothing, cars, and go on vacations, and still there is this emptiness within us that cannot be denied.

The happiness which eludes most of us can only be found within ourselves when we realize there is nothing we don't have. We will find happiness when we have finally reached the level where we are working toward that which we have been created for; our work and purpose on this earth.

When we can do what we love and in that activity can benefit both ourselves and others we will have reached a significant level of fulfillment because we are doing the work which has been intended for us all along.

"Let yourself be

silently drawn

by the stronger

pull of what

you really love."

Rumi

BALANCE YOUR LIFE WITH
WHO YOU LOVE

Balance in life is necessary to having a feeling of well being. We can't spend ten hours a day working and come home and do chores and go to sleep and be leading a healthy life. When we fall into this habit, as I know I have done for years at a time, we begin to feel lost, pessimistic, and alone, like a person enslaved. We can become resentful if we are always giving and never filling up our well with the beauty and the joy of experiencing life with our loved ones.

Take a few moments now to work on this exercise.

*Make a list of the things you would like to do with your partner or best friend. Now write down from that list those which can afford to be done now and write a list of when you will begin to enjoy those new activities with your loved one.

When I did this exercise I wanted to do the following with my husband: study karate, take dance lessons, painting instructions, golf lessons, study a foreign language and feel the freedom of living close to the sea. Since this list was created we have found the time for all of these activities. My husband and I have enjoyed these things together whereas in the past our lives had been moving in different directions.

Decide to construct the life you were created to enjoy. By establishing activities with your loved one you will continue to grow in your appreciation and recognition of one another just as you did when you were first beginning your relationship.

Often when a relationship lasts for a length of time we stop enjoying activities together and pursue our individual interests exclusively. This results in a lack of growth and development in our bond. Just as we develop ourselves by trying new things, so too, do we develop our partnerships by the experiences we share together.

"You give but little

when you give of your possessions.

It is when you give of yourself that

you truly give."

Kahlil Gibran

MAKE SOMEONE
SMILE

"I have found the path of cultivating the awakening mind, the mind which recognizes its' goal as one of aiding other human beings, to be the source of all happiness. It is the way to fulfill our own purpose and the purposes of other sentient beings." The wisdom of the Dalai Lama from his book, <u>The Joy of Living and Dying in Peace</u>.

I want you to do this small exercise before jumping into this section as it will help you in its understanding.

*Write for a few moments about who you make smile during the course of the day. Specify how you go about making others smile.

Write about who makes you smile and how they do that.

Now I want you to meditate on the following quotation for a few moments and see if you can begin to imagine the power in this concept: *"As you travel through life, offer good wishes to each being you meet."* Buddha

Begin today to try this with each and every person you meet. This process can be mind-boggling. The reaction you will get will fill you with joy. What could be better than this? Make someone smile. You can see it in their eyes, the pure pleasure of you recognizing them as someone special. It is truly magical.

To have a feeling of well being; it is important to make someone smile every day. If you are not now doing this then take a moment for this next exercise.

*Make a list of names of the people you touch on a daily basis. Next to each name write something which you could do for them. I am not talking about the big things you might be considering. Once again it is the little things that are important.

Consider things like, paying this person an honest compliment. What might that be for them? Taking notice of what someone is doing. Recognizing someone for the specific performance of his or her job. Showing someone that you appreciate his or her particular abilities.

"At the bottom of things most people want to be understood and appreciated." This is taught to us by the Buddha. How do you feel when you are truly understood and appreciated? It can make all of the difference in the world, can it not?

In the short run if you simply have a mind that wishes to benefit other sentient beings, you will have more courage, your mind will be more relaxed, and the elements of your body will be more in balance. If you take medicine you will more easily digest it. Even a small amount of altruism is like a supreme elixir that overcomes death and its causes. The awakening mind is also like an inexhaustible treasure dispelling the poverty of sentient beings. In the short run it removes poverty when you are within the cycle of existence. Ultimately, all the excellent qualities within the cycle of existence, the state of liberation and Buddhahood are the result of the awakening mind. It is also like a supreme medicine healing sentient beings' sickness. It is like the bright sun removing the murky ignorance of sentient beings." These thoughts are also given to us, by the Dalai Lama.

A quote from the Bodhisatva will help to illuminate this concept further for you.

"May I in all times, temporarily and ultimately, become a protector for those who are without protection. May I become a guide for those who have lost their path, may I become a ship for those who want to cross huge oceans. May I become a bridge for those who want to cross rivers. May I become an island for those who are troubled or in danger at sea. May I become a lamp for those who need light. May I become a place of habitation for those who are looking for shelter. May I become a servant for those who need one. In other words, may I become all those articles that sentient beings need, whatever form they may take. Just like the great elements, earth, water, fire, and air and the space on which they depend, may I become an object of enjoyment for infinite sentient beings. May I become the basis for survival of all sentient beings."

Give yourself a goal of finding something positive to say about every human being you meet each day. This alone can have a dynamic impact on your life. First, if you look for the good in every human being, you will in fact find it. If you tell them that you recognize that good, they will be filled with such appreciation that their behavior throughout the day will be changed because of you. And so every other person that individual touches will, in a way, also be touched by you and your kindness. You see how we can multiply our capacity for goodness simply by recognizing the good in others.

My father lived in the same house for fifty-eight years. This was the house in which we had all grown up. It was filled with many memories both good and bad, but the memories were all ours. The prospect of losing the house was pretty difficult for all of us. But it was most difficult for my father especially because he was ninety-three years old. Mom had died. All of his sisters had passed away. Most of his friends were also gone.

Leaving his house was a very traumatic event. He could no longer live on his own and so he was going to be moving in with my brother where he would have care twenty four hours a day. This was the best possible move that he could make.

I knew this was the best choice for him, although I was saddened to see the old place go. I decided to make the most of it. The last day for Dad and I to be in the house together would be a memorable one.

Prior to the move I had to care for Dad for a couple of days and my concern was that he would be spending the entire time in a state of depression mourning over his terrible fate. To avoid this possibility I created a distraction which he would have never anticipated. While all this was happening during the month of February; I proclaimed that for the next two days, it would be Christmas for us.

I began by going to the Italian deli and buying every traditional Christmas delicacy I could find. Next I went to the crafts store and purchased supplies to create Christmas decorations. After that it was off to the nursery to pick up, you guessed it, a Christmas tree. I found a small indoor tree and took rocks from my father's back yard and dirt from the ground and bark from his tree to fill the container with pieces of his yard.

Next it was off to the frame shop to get a couple of mats and frames for some of the painting I had done which he could hang in his new home. He had always wanted me to bring them for him. I had never felt confident enough to do so since he was a student of the arts and I feared they would not be good enough for him. I was wrong. He was thrilled.

I arrived at my father's house for breakfast and we began with the presentation of the Christmas tree and the announcement that there would be surprises throughout the next two days. As anyone could see, who had eyes to look, it was Christmas!

I had a gift for him to unwrap at every meal and a wonderful delicacy to eat. One surprise after another kept him laughing and giggling throughout the day. I never had so much fun with my father as I did during those two days. Days which I had previously dreaded. It was simply a matter of a change of attitude. We could look at this as horrific or terrific. It was up to us.

At lunchtime we did a little ritual where we took a tin can and a bunch of post-it notes and wrote all of our wonderful memories on them. We folded them neatly and put them into the tin can. We filled the can with all of our great memories and I told Dad he could now bring all of those memories with him to his new house. The idea being that when he got to the new house he could begin to add new memories to the tin can and join them with the old. The memories would never be lost just because we sold the house. They belonged to him and not to his house. His fond old memories would be joined with new wonderful memories. This was not an end but a beginning. This then became an adventure and an opportunity rather than a time of mourning and loss.

I know had I not decided to make this a good time; it would have been a time of tears and sadness instead of laughing and giggling. We got to decide, good or bad, light or dark, pain or joy, it was <u>our</u> decision.

Putting all my energies into making this a wonderful couple of days was a gift I gave myself as well as to Dad. I will never forget the looks on his face throughout these days. How wonderful to make my depressed and hopeless father feel hope and joy again!

"The last of the human freedoms — to choose one's attitude in any given set of circumstances, to choose one's own way."

Viktor Frankl

"Pray to God

But hammer away."

Spanish Proverb

ACTIVE PHILOSOPHY VS.
PASSIVE PHILOSOPHY

I think it is important for you to understand that not all cultures revere the active philosophy. There are many cultures which believe that a passive philosophy is far superior. The reason for this is that the passive philosopher believes an active philosophy has you create missions for yourself and if you do not achieve your objectives you will be miserable and disappointed. The passive philosopher also believes that the active philosopher, even if he attains his goals, will still be unhappy once attaining them. For the passive philosopher, you are probably better off not making any plans and just letting life happen to you.

Active philosophy can be superior if the individual remains fluid in his approach. What I mean by being fluid is to always keep in mind that although you have tremendous power, you are not the *ultimate* power. *Thus you should not grasp on to the results you desire but rather be flexible to the power of the Universe and listen continuously to what your inner voice is telling you about your direction. It is easy for us to abandon hope when things don't go exactly as planned. The forces of the world abound and sometimes we need to remember that the strength of water comes from its ability to take the shape of its environment while always continuing its push forward. Over time a canyon is carved due to the unbeatable combination of both tenacity and flexibility.*

"What the inner voice says will not disappoint the hoping soul"

Schiller

My feelings are that to follow the middle path would be the best choice. Plan for, but do not grasp onto your results. Remain fluid enough to find your way through the barriers you will come up against.

St. Francis of Assisi suggests this active philosophy. Let me be whatever is needed, to help my fellow man:

"Make me an instrument of thy peace. Where there is hatred, let me sow love. Where there is injury, pardon. Where there is doubt, faith. Where there is despair, hope. Where there is darkness, light. Where there is sadness, joy. Oh Divine Master, grant that I may not so much seek to be consoled, as to console; Not so much to be understood, as to understand; Not so much to be loved as to love for it is in giving that we receive. It is in pardoning that we are pardoned. It is in dying that we awaken to the eternal life."

"The fragrance always remains

in the hand that gives the rose."

Gandhi

LET GO OF RESENTMENT

Resentment and hate are barriers to your journey of enlightenment. To become the person you were intended to be it is necessary to put forth all of your energies in a focused direction. When your energies are occupied with resentment and hate your power will be diminished and your path will be blocked.

There is a story about the bandit Angulimal. I think this little tale will aide in your understanding of the concept of working to create, rather than destroy.

When the bandit said he was going to kill the Buddha, the Buddha's reply was; *"Then be good enough to fulfill my dying wish. Cut off the branch of that tree."* One slash of the sword and it was done. *"What next?" asked the bandit. "Put it back again",* said Buddha. *The bandit laughed. "You must be crazy to think that anyone can do that."* **"On the contrary it is you who are crazy to think that you are mighty because you can wound and destroy. That is the task of children. The mighty know how to create and heal."**

When the Dalai Lama accepted the Nobel Peace Prize he said, *"The realization that we are all basically the same human beings, who seek happiness and try to avoid suffering, is very helpful in developing a sense of brotherhood and sisterhood, a warm feeling of love and compassion for others. This in turn is essential if we are to survive in the ever shrinking world we live in. For if we each selfishly pursue only what we believe to be our own interest, without caring about the needs of others we not only may end up harming others, but also ourselves. This fact has become very clear during the course of this century.*

Peace starts within each one of us. When we have inner peace, we can be at peace with those around us. When our community is in a state of peace, it can share that peace with neighboring communities and so on. When we feel love and kindness towards others, it not only makes others feel loved and cared for but it helps us also to develop inner happiness and peace. There are ways in which we can consciously work to develop feelings of love and kindness. For some of us, the most effective way to do so is through religious practice, for others it may be non-religious practice. What is important is that we each make a sincere effort to take seriously our responsibility for each other."

Anger and resentment can be difficult to release. But the process is essential to your personal journey. Be patient with yourself. Be determined to forgive and move in a positive direction, free of the bondage brought about by hate. The following exercise enabled me to shed long held anger which had been holding back my life's progress for years. Once having released the anger a brightness flooded my soul and everything began to fall into its proper place. Forgiving others enabled me to forgive myself.

Begin by placing yourself in a comfortable position as though you were about to meditate. Either sitting or lying down. Relax your body completely. Begin by letting your toes feel limp and move on to allowing your feet to drop with absolute relaxation. Feel how your legs are floating. They are so relaxed, and then your hips and stomach. Enjoy this weightlessness. Your body is in total alignment and you are at peace with your environment. You can notice how your shoulders are letting go and your neck as well feels so soft and supple as does your head and your face. Let your eyes relax and feel the jaw drop open into total relaxation. You are at one with the universe and at peace with the world around you.

"Work of sight is done. Now do heart work on the pictures within you."

Rainer Maria Rilke

Now that you have found the gentleness of this place for your body begin to find the gentle place for your mind as well. Concentrate on your breathing until there is nothing but emptiness. Now it is time to work through the exercise and release the resentment you currently feel.

Bring into your mind the image of the person you wish to forgive. Tell them that you forgive them for all of the difficulties they have brought your way. Tell them you forgive them for all of the sadness they have caused you. Tell them you understand that they are doing the best that they have the ability to do right now and that you understand that as soon as they are able to do better they will be better.

But for now I forgive you for all of the words and thoughts and actions which have caused me pain.

I forgive you. I forgive you. I forgive you.

This is a life changing process. Eliminate all anger, hatred and resentment from your life. The freedom you will feel will lift you up higher than you could have ever imagined. Releasing resentment allows you to soar.

Let go of all feelings of blame and judgment, knowing that you cannot possibly understand everything there is to know about another human being. Without all of that information, you are coming from a place of ignorance when you are so bold as to judge another person.

The person who will be most helped by the releasing of your anger and blame is yourself.

"...Remember that there is only one important time and that is now. The present moment is the only time over which we have dominion. The most important person is always the person you are with, who is right before you, for who knows if you will have dealings with any other person in the future? The most important pursuit is making the person standing at your side happy, for this alone is the pursuit of life."

Leo Tolstoy

ALL MAJOR RELIGIONS

If our major religions are teaching us the same thing; how can we ignore this one unifying force consistent throughout time and from cultures covering the globe? If we can truly understand just one thing about how to best live our lives this must be that one thing.

Buddhism

"Hurt not others with that which pains yourself."

Christianity

"In everything do to others as you would have them

do to you; for this is the law of the prophets."

Confucianism

"Do not impose on others what you

yourself do not desire."

Hinduism

"Never do to others what would pain thyself."

Islam

"Do unto all men as you would they should do unto
   you, and reject for others what you would reject."

Judaism

"What is hateful to you, do not to your fellowmen. That
   is the entire law, all the rest is commentary."

Sikhism

"Treat others as thou wouldst be treated thyself."

Taoism

"Regard your neighbor's gain as your own gain and
   your neighbor's loss as your own loss."

Zoroastrianism

"Do not unto others all that which is not well for
   oneself."

The kindest and gentlest person I have ever known was my Mom. Her love for everyone was unsurpassed in my eyes. I don't remember her ever saying an unkind word. She was the personification of; "Do unto others"...

In 1990 my Mom was diagnosed with pancreatic cancer. She had three months to live. There was nothing that could be done medically to help her.

Although the horror of the experience cannot be denied; there was such a powerful demonstration of love for Mom (from family and friends), which might never have manifested itself without this tragedy. The lessons she taught me were enormous. I shall be forever in her debt for the gift of wisdom she imparted. The courage she showed in the face of such agony was truly heroic.

My brother and sister and I split up the days and lived with Mom in her home for the three months prior to her death. I remember her telling me that she had lead a wonderful life and that it was her time for something like this just as those who had gone before her had gone through such crises.

She seemed so accepting of her fate that she almost eased into it. Physically the illness was a cruel and savage monster to my gentle mother. It ravaged her body. I can remember her telling me that she could hardly believe the human body could endure such brutality.

It was strange how her body was so destroyed but her beauty remained untouched. In fact, I can say quite honestly that she was more beautiful during that time than I had ever seen her. It was almost as if her inner soul could be seen on the outside.

One of our most important moments came when I asked if I could lie down in bed next to her and just be there with her. I told her how strong I thought she was because of the way she had lived her life. She smiled and said, "Really, do you think I am strong, really?" I'll never forget that smile she gave me in the midst of her great pain. She was so happy to know that I understood and recognized her for who she was and for what she had endured over the years with such grace and beauty.

"Do unto others as you would have others do unto you."

Recognize the greatness of the others around you and let them know that you appreciate who they are at their center. This recognition and appreciation will fill both the giver and the receiver with joy.

"When you are content to be

simply yourself

and don't compare or compete,

everybody will respect you."

Lao-Tzu

GOOD TO KNOW YOU
ARE NOT ALONE

Before deciding exactly which questions to ask for this work, I spent several years interviewing people from different backgrounds. I wanted to understand which questions needed to be asked. I wanted to watch as the light went on in their minds and see where that light would take them. It is illuminating to read some of their answers, and thus gain a more profound appreciation for the fact that we are all in this together...

****

This first individual understood the value of creating a healthy lifestyle. She finds joy in her work, puts exercise into her life in a sport she loves, spends time with her children (which is a priority) and lets herself go to hell once in a while.

Although not everyone would have judged her successful I have deemed her to be because of her belief in herself and her ability to know that whatever challenges her she can handle. I think she was successful because she was happy with the life she had created for herself. Her professional life brought joy to others as well.

When asked, "How have you been kind to yourself this week?" her reply was the following:

"I took a nice long bath, stayed in bed during the cold days. I played tennis. I went out to lunch with a friend and enjoyed a crafts fair. This is a good time for me. I am on vacation from the market, so I plan fun things every day. I even get to spend a day with my daughter every week. When I play tennis with my friend we laugh for an entire hour. I have been sure to put joy into every week. Even when I work I enjoy it. I get great joy on those days when it is bitter cold and I can stay home and watch soaps because I have completed my work. That is a good thing to do, not everyday but once in a while."

Sometimes life sets up barriers to our work and we find ourselves in a holding pattern, just waiting until the traffic clears before we begin. His response to the question, "What do you need to do to improve yourself?" was the following:

"I need to commit myself to a period of time to make the improvement happen, rather than putting it off because I don't know where I am going to be. I don't have any long-term goals. I think that one day I will make those plans but not right now."

"What have been your peak experiences in life?"

"Having my children, getting married, seeing my girls get degrees, losing my mother, finding out she was sick, finding out I was pregnant."

This person answered with the simplest of responses. What would make you happier?

"A good nap and my down comforter."

"It would be fun to have nicer things but at what cost, if its going to jeopardize your health or deny your children, what have you got?"

"I would like to feel myself moving forward toward my goals in life. Right now I feel like I am in limbo, treading water, not going forward. I'm happy with everything in my life except myself. I don't know how great your life can be, if you are not happy with the way you are. A lot of things about me I would like to change. If you like yourself you're happy. No matter how great your life is if you don't like yourself it's a real problem. I do like myself but I feel like I am a work in progress, I want to go faster to my goals."

When asked if she was afraid of death, this woman's answer was one of the funniest.

"I pray to die healthy. I don't want to die of some horrendous illness, so I stay healthy. I also don't want to die naked. I want to die healthy and not nude."

This next person was letting fear inhibit action in life. Consider how many times you have done the same thing and then ask yourself how you might replace fear with faith.

"I am terrified of death, if I don't think about it I am ok. I feel like a lot of my life has been wasted. I feel like I am just waking up and so it makes me feel impatient and worried I won't get things done. It makes me feel I might make a mistake, so I don't do anything because

I might do it wrong. I don't want to lie on my deathbed at ninety and have regrets. I've got one chance and I don't want to screw it up. When I do something I want to do it wholeheartedly."

To become all you were intended to be, it is necessary to have identified both your strengths and your weaknesses.

"Strengths, I don't have any." There was a very long pause before she was able to identify her strengths. "Well, I am a good friend. I am low key. I don't get angry a lot. I try to look at things in a certain way. I try and look at the good. I am a good parent, not too firm.

I wrote a poem for my boss when he retired and it was wonderful and I was proud of myself and I read it at his retirement party and one part really got to everybody, "A world full of knowledge, so much more to inspire, I just have one question, do you have to retire?"

I wrote ten verses and I framed it for him. I was nervous because I don't like how I sound. But it came out perfect, and everyone said it was beautiful and he was so happy.

I liked doing this, but it doesn't come naturally, and it took a lot of time and I had to be totally happy about what I wrote. People at work asked for a copy of it. It made me feel so good about myself. I was so glad I did a good job and it was me."

Notice how her strengths are shown in relationships and accomplishments. Also note how she put her complete self into the work until it became her. The work was rewarding because it benefited both herself and others.

"This is not what I really want to do. This sounds so trite, but I don't know who I am. I spent my whole life married to my kids and now I don't know who I am. I have too much freedom. I don't have to work right now. I have no pressure to do something now. What makes me happy is being with people. Right now I don't have people in my life at all. I get bored very easily. I don't know where I get this from, except I am a perfectionist. I wouldn't want a job alone at a desk. The problem is I am always looking to do what is right for everybody else but for me. So I was studying geology, because of my husband's business, but that is not what I really want to do. I don't know who I am."

What kind of barriers have you created which impede your progress?

"All I seem to be able to see are the things which can not be. I never seem to be able to see clear to all that is possible for me. I just cannot see what others seem to be able to see. It is as though I wear blinders, or maybe everyone else is wearing blinders."

"My poor sense of direction has kept me from being the best I could be. It costs me and limits me in exploring anything other than my own little world. It prevented me from visiting my mom, when she lived in New York and I was in New Jersey and I can't bring that back, I would wait for once a month to go and see her with my husband."

Consider the barriers you have erected in your life and work to eliminate them one at a time.

At the conclusion of one of the interviews the person discovered the following:

"I wouldn't normally say I was a most fulfilled person and yet talking to you I guess I am. I am a simple person. The things I wanted I earned and bought for myself. If I want something I will get it, but what is important to me is the grass roots stuff. I don't want diamonds and fancy cars and shopping trips every day. I am not looking for anything that I don't have. Some people are never going to be satisfied. I am satisfied with the basic things. I am a successful person."

Happiness doesn't come from getting more but from wanting less.

Have you lived your life in your own way?

"I have never done what I wanted to do because only a selfish person would do that. I have always done what I needed to do for my family."

"I guess as much as is possible when you have a family and responsibility but I think I pretty much love it all and always have. There was a time when for so many years I gave much too much to my employer, but I have learned what is to be valued and the dollar is just not it. Granted you need enough to be comfortable but after that it is all just gravy."

If you had no fear what would you do now?

"No fears have inhibited my behavior as much as responsibilities have. I would do things differently if I didn't have a family to care for but not because of fear. Maybe I don't like to fly and am afraid of that but it doesn't keep me from going on vacation. I just don't plan on becoming a flight attendant."

"I would go back to school if I were not afraid of failing."

"I would be myself."

"I would change my career to something I love."

What gets in the way of your being the best you can be?

"My weight. I have struggled with it my entire life."

This person wasn't any more than ten pounds overweight and yet they were letting this have such impact on their self-image. Consider if you are doing the same thing to yourself in one way or another. Sometimes we put much too much importance on something as benign as a couple of pounds.

What would you do if you had just a year to live?

"I would live my life exactly as I wished to live it. I would move to the place I have always wanted to live. I would make time for my family and friends. I would have them over whenever they could make it and be available to them whenever they needed my help.

I would steep myself in all of the books I have not yet gotten to read. I would delight in the most wonderful food I could possibly find. I would take in every sunset and every sunrise. I would tell my husband how much I love and appreciate who he is and all that he has done to help me along this road. In fact I would tell everyone in my life how much I love them and what I appreciate about them.

I think the value of going that extra step is something I have missed doing over the years and would make all the difference in the world in the lives of the people I love. They should understand not only that I love them but that I appreciate them for who they are and understand them.

I would laugh a lot. I know that sounds silly considering the end is near but I think it would be appropriate if I was finally doing what I had always wanted to be doing."

Take a look at your answer to this question. Ask yourself; "If not now then when?"

If you could have dinner with one person, living or dead, who would it be and what would you talk about?

"I would want to have a dinner party and invite Moses, Jesus, Buddha, and Mohammed. I would want them to have a conversation about their similarities and their differences and I would be a fly on the wall and watch and listen and learn.

I would ask them what could be done to bring the people of the world together in love and stop the hatred and the wars in the name of religion and prejudice and greed and righteousness."

What are your deepest desires?

"I want my husband to understand who I am and what is important to me. I have tried to tell him about what is of value to me but he just doesn't seem to get it. I sometimes cry because it seems as though we see life in such a different light. It is almost as if we are not living in the same universe. If only he could know who I am and appreciate me for my beliefs. That would make me the happiest person in the world."

Do you like yourself? What don't you like about yourself and what do you like about yourself?

"I like when I am at peace with myself and with others. I don't like it when I am agitated with my performance and the performance of others. I like that I am patient and understanding, and that I enjoy the simple things in life. Looking at nature can make me smile for hours on end. Reading a good book can keep me smiling for days. I like that I enjoy helping my friends and that they come to me for help. I like that I can listen to others with empathy and usually make them feel comfortable enough to speak with me. I like that I have the courage to do what others may think is foolish.

I don't like my inability to be free from concern of what others think. I know that this is foolish and yet my behavior shows that I am unable to put into practice what I know to be true. I don't like it when I am not disciplined. I feel that self governess is necessary to bring my qualities to the surface but get angry with myself when I don't do what I know is best for me."

Do you wish your life were different? What are you doing about making the changes in your life that you feel are important?

"I hate my life the way it is right now and I want it to be different but I don't seem to be able to take the steps needed to get me out of the situation I am currently in.

I find the work I am doing to be a drudge and yet I have no choice but to keep on doing it because I need the money. I know I can get another job but I would probably hate that as much as I hate this. I work fifty hours a week and have no time for anything other than work. I do nothing for myself at all. I don't even want to do anything.

I have thought about starting a new business but don't seem to find the time to get the thing off the ground. I know that I will never change this life if I don't start to take action but I have not been able to do so."

What do you need for balance?

"I need time for myself. I need time to exercise every day and time to read in peace and quiet. I need good conversation with friends and family. I need to keep in contact with the spiritual side of life. I need good work. I need to be needed by others. I need beauty and order in my life. I need to be loved and to love."

Can you rely upon yourself to get things done?

"I have a tendency to procrastinate things and so I sometimes need others to give me a push to get things done. I need the support of my friends to help me through in many areas of my life. I think the older I get the more rigid I become and the more I need others to help me to see what is possible. I get hung up on unimportant issues and need help to get beyond them to move ahead."

*Answer each of these questions for yourself. Reflect on your answers and how they relate to the answers given by those interviewed.

Know that you are not alone. We are all here struggling to make the most of the gifts we have been given. We are all doing the best we can.

Remember to have compassion for all of those "others" as they are dealing with their own obstacles just as you are dealing with yours.

"Keep your face

to the sunshine

and you can not

see the shadow."

Helen Keller

THE BEGINNING

<u>CHAPTER TWELVE</u>

MISSION STATEMENT

DAILY PRAYER

LIST OF REMINDERS

BOOKS TO READ ALONG THE WAY

CONCLUSION

"Continue to live with

this high goal in view,

and you will remain

in perfect peace."

Augustine

MISSION STATEMENT

Once you have decided where you are today and where you wish to go in this life; you have the basics needed to write your personal mission statement.

The idea is to read your mission statement every morning and every evening so you are certain to create a day, which will carry you closer to the purpose of your life. If at the end of your day you realize you did nothing to advance your purpose you can reaffirm your commitment for the next morning.

Here are a couple of questions to ask yourself to help give you a few more ideas for writing this mission:

*Think about how you might positively impact the lives of others. When you look around, what makes you crazy? What do you love to do? What are you passionate about? What can you do to create positive change in these areas?

Your objective is to create a mission statement which is as simple as possible. Make the statement as brief as you are able to while still getting at the essence of the thing. The mission will be easiest to accomplish if it is written in clear and simple language.

To help you with your mission I will share what I have developed as my personal mission statement. I have spent most of my life working on this problem but didn't notice until several years ago that that is what I was doing, and what I wanted to do consciously rather than unconsciously.

What I would find as I visited with so many of the people who worked for our organization, was that many of them had locked themselves into places they hated. What I saw constantly were wonderful, talented, and frustrated people who had talents far greater than they themselves had the ability to see. By listening to so many stories and doing what I could to counsel these people, the picture of my life's mission gradually became more clear to me. Eventually the light went on for me and I realized my life's mission was; "To help others to see their own light."

"My function in life was to render clear what was already blindingly conspicuous."

Quentin Crisp

"Your lamp was

lit from another

lamp. All God wants

is your gratitude for that."

Rumi

DAILY PRAYER

Once you have established your mission statement it is a good idea to now create your own personal prayer to say every day. This is a way to keep you on track. You will find that if you start each and every day with this prayer, it will remind you of your mission and the fact that the only way to get to that mission is by the work you do today.

I also suggest that at the end of every day you repeat your personal prayer as a means of summoning up your mission once again. If the work of the day was not moving you in the direction of your life's mission, you can take note of that fact and start fresh tomorrow.

The purpose of the prayer is to keep you focused and on the path which you have created for yourself. The prayer will keep you aware and awake and prevent you from wandering off in other directions.

I have included my daily prayer as a way of showing you the simplicity of the approach.

"HELP OTHERS TO SEE THEIR OWN LIGHT"

THY WILL BE DONE.

GIVE ME THE STRENGTH TO FOLLOW THE WAY.

GIVE ME THE COURAGE TO NOT BACK DOWN.

GIVE ME THE VISION TO RECOGNIZE THE POWER WITHIN.

GIVE ME THE ABILITY TO SEE THE POTENTIAL.

LET ME REALIZE THE DREAM YOU HAVE DREAMED FOR ME.

THY WILL BE DONE.

HELP OTHERS TO SEE THEIR OWN LIGHT.

"If you take care

of each moment

you will take care

of all time."

Buddha

Daily List of Reminders

Do something for someone else.
Forgive others and forgive yourself.
Surprise yourself by doing something out of the ordinary.
Make someone smile.
Treat yourself to one act of kindness.
Tell yourself you are valuable to the world.
Do your exercises.
Nourish your body with healthy foods.
Read something wonderful to nourish your mind.
Thank your Creator for something that happened today.
Tell and show someone you love them.
Say your life's mission out loud.
Quiet yourself long enough to listen to the voice within.
Pay attention to what you love.
Choose to live as if this is your last day on earth.

Tear this page out and post it where you will see it first thing every morning. Review your list at the beginning and end of the day to be sure nothing has been missed. Following these simple steps will create the environment for your most dynamic growth toward the fullness of your potential.

BOOKS TO READ ALONG THE WAY

Babitt by Sinclair Lewis
The Souls Code by James Hillman
The Fall by Albert Camus
Treatise on Happiness by Thomas Aquinas
Socrates, Buddha, Confusious, Jesus by Karl Jaspers
Meister Eckhart selected writings by Davis
The Prophet by Kahlil Gibran
The Gospel According to the Son by Norman Mailer
The Tibetan Book of Living and Dying by Rinpoche
Genesis a New Translation by Stephen Mitchell
Thoughts on the East by Thomas Merton
The Complete Works of Joseph Campbell
The Tao Te Ching by Lao Tzu
The Joy of Living and Dying in Peace by the Dalai Lama
Poems of St. John of the Cross translated by W.Barnstone
No Greater Love by Mother Teresa
Siddartha by Hermann Hesse
A Year to Live by Stephen Levine
Claiming Your Self-Esteem by Carolyn Ball
Spiritual Literacy by Fred and Maryann Brussat
How Then Shall We Live? by Wayne Muller
Soul Mates by Thomas Moore
Immortality by Milan Kundera
The Seven Story Mountain by Thomas Merton
Something of a Rebel by William Shannon
A Parliament of Souls by Tobias, Morrison, Gray
Flow and Creativity by Mihaly Csikszentmihalyi
The Allegory of the Cave by Plato
Ishmael by Daniel Quinn
Joshua by Joseph Girzone

"Our deepest fears

are like dragons

guarding our

deepest treasure."

Rainer Maria Rilke

CONCLUSION

We have covered so much territory, in so little time. I am feeling exhausted for all of you. But I know that your journey, just like mine, is not ending with the conclusion of this book. I know that you are on the brink of a new beginning.

Rather than being overwhelmed, I expect you are in a state of relaxation and contentment, knowing now for the first time that you have everything you need within yourself. There is nothing lacking in any of you that cannot be found by taking this journey inside of yourself to the deepest places where the essence of you lies just waiting to be experienced.

You are joy and light, order and beauty, love and glory. You are all of the most wonderful things you can begin to imagine and so much more than you can ever perceive.

I remain in awe of who you are and from where you have come. Love one another and watch your acorn grow with colors so spectacular it will take your breath away.

"There is no way of telling people that they are all walking around shining like the sun."

Thomas Merton

ABOUT THE AUTHOR

As a personal development coach, public speaker, corporate trainer and business manager, Susan George has worked for thirty years teaching others to think beyond their self-imposed limits. She has taught her audiences and employees alike how to tap into their power within and the vast world of unexplored possibilities which lie before them waiting for their acknowledgement.

She continues with this book and her seminars to spread the word of opportunity and the path to attain your desires through thought, investigation, dedication, meditation, application, and inspiration.

Her mantra is simple; you are able to be and do far more than you have ever imagined. The core of her philosophy is by discovering who you are and your purpose, you will begin to experience the life of your dreams. The light you have to give this world has enormous value and worth and begs to be shared so that both you and others will experience the joy you were meant to feel as a participant on this most magnificent journey.

Because Susan sees the essence of the individual she offers a window through which to see your unique potential. Using the Socratic method and ideas from many great minds throughout history as tools to cleanse the dust from that window, Susan gently guides you to see your true self for the very first time.

*

For information about tapes, books, seminars or newsletters:

Phone – 732-282-0220

Fax – 732-282-0330

e-mail: sgeorge@servicexcel.com